THE ONLY ONE LIVING TO TELL

The Only One Living to Tell

THE AUTOBIOGRAPHY OF A YAVAPAI INDIAN

Mike Burns

EDITED BY Gregory McNamee

THE UNIVERSITY OF
ARIZONA PRESS

TUCSON

THE UNIVERSITY OF ARIZONA PRESS

www.uapress.arizona.edu

Library of Congress Cataloging-in-Publication Data
Burns, Mike, 1865?–1934.
    The only one living to tell : the autobiography of a Yavapai indian /
Mike Burns ; edited by Gregory McNamee.
        p. cm.
    Includes bibliographical references.
    ISBN 978-0-8165-0120-5 (pbk. : alk. paper)
    1. Burns, Mike, 1865?–1934.   2. Yavapai Indians—Biography.   3. Yavapai
Indians—History.   I. McNamee, Gregory.   II. Title.
    E99.Y5B874 2012
    305.897'5724—dc23   2011046513

Publication of this book is made possible in part by the proceeds of a permanent
endowment created with the assistance of a Challenge Grant from the National
Endowment for the Humanities, a federal agency.

Preface

A few days before Christmas of 1872, a hundred-odd miles to the north and east of what is now Phoenix, Arizona, advance scouts of a force of American soldiers, the vanguard of the military campaign that launched the Apache Wars, captured a young Indian boy about eight or ten years old. The boy had been looking for a missing horse with his uncle, who, it seems, abandoned him at the enemy's approach. Alone, freezing, the boy waited to be killed, for that was the way of the bluecoats. Instead, the scouts, whom army rolls listed as "Tonto Apaches"—*tonto* coming from the Spanish word for "fool" or "idiot" and apparently an insult used by other Indians in reference to collaborators—terrified their young captive into revealing the whereabouts of his family, who were hiding in the safety of the Salt River Canyon. Within a few days, the time it took the American soldiers to pick their way through the rugged mountains to reach the remote *ranchería*, Hoomothya, "Wet Nose," was an orphan.

The people the Americans found there were Kwevkepayas, members of one of the four far-flung tribal branches that would eventually be subsumed under the name "Yavapai." About a hundred of these Kwevkepayas were sheltering under a rock overhang in a canyon above the Salt River when some hundred and twenty soldiers, accompanied by more than a hundred Akimel O'odham (Pima) and Maricopa auxiliaries and a small detachment of Tonto Apache scouts, attacked. The soldiers rained fire from across the canyon, ricocheting bullets from the roof to cut down the sheltered defenders. An American commander, Capt. James Burns, ordered that boulders be rolled down from above the cave to crush other Kwevkepayas. When the shooting stopped, the Akimel O'odham advanced, crushing the skulls of the dying with rifle butts and rocks. Some seventy-six Kwevkepayas died. Hoomothya's father, two younger siblings, aunts, uncles, cousins, and grandfather were among the dead of what became known as the Battle of the Caves, which an eyewitness, an officer named John Gregory Bourke, called "the most signal blow ever received by the Apaches in Arizona." History now knows the event as the Skeleton Cave Massacre, a more accurate term, since the so-called battle was decidedly one-sided: one Akimel O'odham fighter died, but otherwise the attacking force did not suffer a single casualty.

The Kwevkepayas had ranged across much of the central Arizona highlands for generations, ever since their ancestors moved eastward from the Colorado River country in search of game and a place where fewer enemies lived. Their luck ran out with the arrival of the Americans, who, beginning in the 1860s, effectively declared war on the indigenous peoples of the region, most of whom they collectively called "Apaches," although only the easternmost of the peoples of the high country were true Apaches, Athapaskans who had migrated into Arizona from far north hundreds of years earlier. The Kwevkepayas and their cousins, the Tolkepayas, were variously known as Apache Mohaves (or Mojaves), Mohave (or Mojave) Apaches, and Yuma Apaches; the Tontos were Yavapais who lived in the Mogollon Rim country near the Verde River and present-day Payson. After 1865, when a mining boom drew hundreds of whites to the region near Prescott and Jerome, no ethnographic niceties were ventured. All Indians became Apaches, and all Apaches became targets.

James Burns took Hoomothya, whom he called Mickey or Mike, into his household as something between ward and servant, and there Mike Burns remained for several months, until the captain took ill and left for Washington, leaving it to his family to follow him. The boy's duties were several: he mucked the stables, cleaned the house, shined boots, did odd jobs—and, it appears, was dispatched to spy on Yavapais interned near Fort Whipple, witnessing their destruction as one band after another surrendered before the promise of reservations near their highlands homeland.

The promise was not honored. No American officer ever expected that it would be, and the Yavapais were soon relocated to the much-hated San Carlos Reservation along the Gila River in southeastern Arizona. Mike was by this time the charge of a man who would become something of a foster father to him, Capt. Hall S. Bishop, and for the next few years he and Bishop would cross the western frontier, fighting many Indian nations and accumulating adventures that, as Mike relates them in this autobiography, sometimes verge on the improbable—and sometimes even unbelievable.

Mike Burns lived in two worlds, and he was at home in neither. The whites alongside whom he served as an army scout and later in various roles never saw him as anything other than an Indian, which was no good thing in the late nineteenth and early twentieth centuries. Uprooted and without kin, Mike had only tenuous contact with his own people for many years. Only in his twenties, when he married, did he hear his own language regularly spoken; only then did he receive an education in Kwevkepaya and Tolkepaya lifeways from his in-laws and neighbors. Until his death in 1934 he continued to gather material about his people's beliefs and history, making notes such as this: "To know all the names of the ranges of mountains and peaks: the noted Superstition Mountains are called by the Indians Wee-git-a-sour-ha, 'a rock looking up.' Wee-ga-jaide-haw is the mountain called Four Peaks. We call the Salt River Ah-haw-gith-e-la."

Mike tried at several points to publish his historical and ethnographic pieces, turning to help where he could, as he did with one correspondent, a well-meaning schoolteacher: "This is all I can say just now, but if you need more, or if you can get someone who would be interested in what I write, I wish you would tell me so. I need help all the time, as you know; I am an Indian, and I have a large family, and I am the only one now living to look after my children. Please let me hear from you soon. Good-bye, Miss Ruth Arnold. I am a lonely Indian." Alas, Miss Arnold could do nothing, it appears, to fulfill Mike's dream of presenting the lives of his people from—that anthropological desideratum above all others—the native point of view. Neither, as we will see, could anyone else of his own time. At least, no one did.

The memoir that you hold in your hands likewise inhabits the space between two worlds. Written originally in a language that is not quite English, interspersed with grammatical constructions that are not quite Yavapai, Burns's autobiography, most of which takes place in the fourteen tumultuous years from 1872 to 1886, follows a path as circuitous as the history Burns relates.

Mike Burns at about the
age of forty.

Unlike so many Native American memoirs and autobiographies
before our own time, Mike Burns's story is not an "as told to" account, not filtered for audiences that expected to find their precon-
ceptions about history and Native life reinforced. Armed with a type-
writer, Burns set forth a story that is rightly full of indignation and
complaint at the treatment that his people had suffered—but more
that he, as a person unmoored from his culture and thrust into another, had been made to endure. Even today, more than eighty years
after Burns finished writing his story, his condemnations are scorch-
ing and discomfiting, and if Burns often seems self-pitying, there is
no doubt that he more than earned the right to criticize the dominant
Anglo-American society even as he worked, as a scout, to make the
Arizona frontier safe for its ascension.

I have tried to put Mike's experiences into the ordinary English
of his time, careful to use only words that he himself used. I have
restructured some of the lesser episodes and tried to give chronologi-
cal coherence to the whole, but I have also retained many of Burns's
pauses, false starts, and sometimes circular storytelling in the spirit of
Morris Opler's approach to the Mescalero Apache author of the book
Opler called *Apache Odyssey*: "The narrator was allowed to emphasize,
embellish, and ignore as he chose, for it was felt that the degree to
which he developed a subject was an index of his emotional invest-

ment in it." By that token, it soon becomes clear what Mike Burns wished to remember: the murder of his people and their continued mistreatment at white hands, something that white audiences of the time had very little interest in hearing.

Opler also observed, rightly, that "the Mescalero, as is the case with many other American Indian groups, are well aware that the Western history that the white man has written has much to say about Indian 'atrocities' but has passed very lightly over the cruelties suffered by the Indians at the hands of their white antagonists." Just so, Thomas Edwin Farish, the distinguished historian of early Arizona, published portions of Mike's reminiscences—though considerably toned down, it should be said, by a contemporary editor who, for whatever reason, was inclined to accept official explanations concerning murder, atrocity, robbery, and other crimes against humanity. For all that, Farish was impressed:

> So much has been written of the Indians by the white man, so many reports have been made by the military and other authorities, of the massacres by the red men, and so little is known of the Indian's side of the story, that the following stories of the Apache Indians, written by one of themselves, Mike Burns, will, without doubt, cast a new light on the question, not only for Indian account of many battles with the white man, but also for description of the methods of travel and customs and manner of living of the Indians. It is a pathetic narrative, elegant in its simplicity, and shows the deep feeling of an Indian brooding over the wrongs which he has received at the hands of the whites. It is an eloquent appeal for justice at the hands of those who took from him his lands and robbed him of friends and relatives. . . .
> I think many parts of it will rank with the orations of Red Fox, Black Hawk and other Indians who have made their names a part of the history of this country.

Generations after his death, Mike Burns finally has a chance to make that appeal for justice, a chance to tell his story. Like Herodotus, he was not always on hand to witness the events he describes. He did not share in all the suffering of his people, but he asked the right and necessary questions and delivered compelling answers. He may not always have been on hand when and where he said he was—but then again, we have no good reason to disbelieve anything he says, at least not on the largest scale.

Mike Burns documents, on a personal scale, a record of broken promises that, on the larger scale, so sharply characterizes the history of Indian-white relations across time. In doing so, he provides a view of Arizona history, of Native American history, that we would otherwise not have, and he complicates our view of life on the nineteenth-century frontier, joining the voices of Sarah Winnemucca, Geronimo, Ishi, and other chroniclers of the Native past. He is a necessary witness whose account helps us come to terms with an almost incomprehensible history, and he has an extraordinary tale to tell.

— Gregory McNamee

THE ONLY ONE LIVING TO TELL

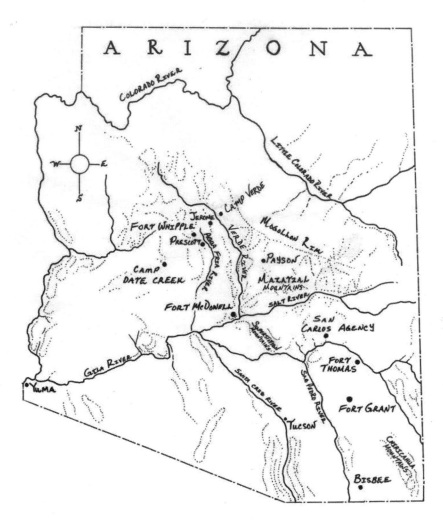

I

I cannot say exactly when or where I was born, because I belonged to an Apache Indian family whose parents were not educated, so that I could not find any records of my birthplace. Only educated people keep records of their children so that they can know where they were born, and besides, there are no older Indians left alive now. All of my people were killed by the soldiers and by Indian scouts who worked for the government. This was in 1872, in a cave on the north side of the Salt River, where about 225 souls—men, women, and poor innocent children—were living. The place is on the north side of the mouth of Fish Creek on the Salt River, where Horseshoe Dam is now.

I left that camp a few days before the slaughter, traveling north with an old man, my uncle, and a horse that carried me on its back. We were overtaken by soldiers in the middle of the night, and I was left alone when my uncle ran away. I got in a rock hole and stayed there all night without any clothes or blankets. The Four Peaks were white with snow, and I was only a few miles away from them. How I got through that freezing night is a miracle. In the morning about sunup I came out of the hole. I had been listening through the night to see if there were any enemies close by, but I could not hear a thing, so I crawled out from a different entrance from the one I entered and went up to a little hill overlooking the countryside. My uncle and I had built a camp the previous night, with a fire to lie beside, but now there were many men in blue clothing there.

They made a rush for me. I didn't move, and they came and caught hold of my little arm. They pulled me over rocks and bushes. The men didn't care whether I got hurt or not. The rest of the soldiers were looking for more Indians over the hill, but when they found none they joined us. I was taken to an officer, Captain James Burns of the Fifth US Cavalry. This all happened on December 22, 1872, a date recorded by Lieutenant E. D. Thomas, who was under Captain

Burns's command. They were from Fort McDowell, the place where I am living now.

It is a mysterious thing, the fact that I am alive to tell how I was saved, while every last one of my tribe was killed. I can only guess that I was born in 1864, because Lieutenant Thomas told me that on the day I was captured he reckoned me to be seven or eight years old. That would make me sixty-six years old now, though I know that I am older than that because I know many things from way back. I can remember when my mother was killed by soldiers a few miles east of Mormon Flat. She ran for her life and crawled into a rock hole, too, and she was pulled out and shot many times. I then had two children to take care of, a little brother and a baby sister. I remember that as if it had happened just a short time ago. It was an awful day for me after I lost my poor mother and had to look after two children. My aunt had a baby, and so that way my little sister was nursed.

From that time on my father had a bitter hatred for soldiers and all white people. My father and others would go down into the Salt River Valley looking for soldiers or white men to kill.

Once they brought seven or eight ponies into our camp, and they gave one to another man whose camp was beyond the Four Peaks to the north. I was away from our camp at the time. Then soldiers came, and they captured thirty-two women and children and brought them to Fort McDowell, somewhere in the last part of December 1872. The prisoners were taken in wagons across the desert to Florence and then to old Fort Grant on the San Pedro River. A few weeks later the command moved nearer the Superstition and Pinal Mountains, coming across the country to where Globe is now—this was before the town was built—and then on to the San Carlos River, before the San Carlos Agency was established. Then they went on to Fort Thomas and to a newly established post that was also called Fort Grant.

Early in the spring of 1873, the soldiers marched back to San Carlos. Captain Burns commanded G Troop of the Fifth Cavalry, and Captain Price commanded F Troop. The two commands moved north from Globe along the Salt River to where Roosevelt Dam now is, then followed Tonto Creek and on to where Payson is now located, crossed the East Verde River, traveled several days, and reached Camp Verde. The soldiers moved on to Fort Whipple, and then G Troop went west to Camp Date Creek.

The Indian agency at Camp Verde, Arizona, to which the US Army removed several Yavapai groups from 1865 to 1890.

At that post were many Indians from the west, including Yumas who had come to make a treaty with the soldiers. The Indians remained there for a few weeks, then were moved on to Camp Verde and Cottonwood, about twenty-five miles away. Nearly all of the Yavapais and Tonto Apaches came to Camp Verde to make a treaty with General George Crook, who was commanding the Department of Arizona. General Crook had been friendly, and he told them that they could make their homes in the Verde Valley for as long as they lived. But only a year later General Crook gathered all the Indians and told them that they had to move to the San Carlos Agency. About 3,500 people moved.

In the spring of 1874 Captain Burns and G Company went to Fort Whipple. In 1875 the regiment changed departments, so that the Sixth Cavalry was to come to Arizona and the Fifth was to take its place in the Indian Territory. G Company moved in the early part of July, reaching Camp Verde on the day before the Fourth of July, when many soldiers got drunk. They reached their new station in October. I was with them for eight years, although Captain Burns himself died at Navajo Spring in 1874.

Captain Burns's and Captain Price's companies reached them at the rim of the cave. This was a different camp from the one where I had left my grandpa and little brother and sister, who was now about three years old, and my aunt with her five children. It brings tears to my eyes to remember them, for they were all slaughtered there with 225 others, men, women, and children, and along with them the great chief Delshe, who was killed when he told the Indians to get behind the big rocks that stood at the front of the cave, so that the soldiers could not see them.

One soldier had me by the arm, just tumbling me over the bushes and the rocks. He didn't care whether I was hurt or killed; he took me along just like he was dragging a log.

Most of the soldiers, about six hundred of them, were on a three-hundred-foot-tall cliff at the east corner of the cave. They could not see the Indians. Delshe had said that no enemy would dare attack there because it was such a fortified place. The Indians thought that they were strongly protected, but then the soldiers shot down volleys, bucketsful of lead behind the big boulders against the walls of the cave, pouring down such showers of lead that those whom the bullets hit could not be recognized as humans. The war songs ceased. Only one man was left, and he had just one shot remaining, and with it he killed a Pima Indian scout, right at noon. He might have killed more, but when he reached out with his gun to drag over bullets or a bag of gunpowder, the soldiers fired, and their shots bent his gun nearly in two. He was helpless, and then he was finally shot. He was my brother-in-law, a man who never missed a shot, and he died like a man.

The Pima and Maricopa scouts rushed in and killed any Indians who were still alive. They pounded their heads in right in front of the soldiers. Some Apache scouts who were with the soldiers found some women and children alive, and they handed them over to the officers for fear that the Pimas and Maricopas would get them too, so enraged were they, even though just one of their number got killed that day.

They weren't satisfied with killing more than two hundred men, women, and innocent children. They gathered about thirty of the wounded and killed them too.

Some Apache scouts had fired warning shots before the soldiers arrived. If Delshe's band had rushed out of the cave when they heard them, they would not have been slaughtered. A few feeble old men and women might have been killed, but Chief Delshe urged everyone

Pakakiwa, son-in-law of the Kwevkepaya leader Delshe.

not to make a break for it. Most of the Indians were depending on the old chief because he had been a great warrior and had fought all kinds of people, and he had always come out victorious when he fought against soldiers and Pimas. This time he was pinned down and surrounded, and he could not protect his people.

After the last of the Yavapais were killed, I was led into the cave. I saw dead men and women lying around in all shapes, horrid to look on. I saw where my grandpa lay; I saw at a distance a body that was in a little rock hole, headfirst, and that was the old man. I was at the west entrance of the cave and sat there crying to death. Then I thought of my little brother and sister, the two I cared for and fed as a mother would. No more hope, no more kinfolk in the world. What would I do? Should I give myself up to the Pimas and Maricopas to be killed there with my family? Should I forget those awful deeds against my people and take on a new and manly courage, resolve to be a different man and hope for a better future?

The Pimas and Maricopas had gathered around their dead friend and were crying harder than I was. I thought it best to stop crying while these big men were crying, lest some of them come and beat me with their clubs. The Pimas and Maricopas carried the body away. None of the soldiers or officers or Apache scouts were hurt. Afterward I heard that one soldier got shot in his hat, close to his head, but that was the only near-injury among the hundreds of soldiers.

In all history no civilized race has murdered another as the American soldiers did my people in the year 1872. They slaughtered men, women, and children without mercy, as if they were not human. I am the only one living to tell what happened to my people.

2

The slaughter of my people ended at about four in the afternoon. The soldiers took the captives up to the top of the cave and marched the Indians in front of them, and the Apache scouts were warned to keep close watch so that the Pimas and Maricopas did not slip in and kill the women and children before we knew it. There was one woman who was so badly wounded that she could not get on a horse, and so she was left there. Some soldiers gave her food and water, but as soon as they were out of sight some Pimas went back and mashed her head to jelly. They hated the Apaches.

It happened that six young women had gotten away from the cave before daybreak that morning. They were saved, unhurt. One of them was a young grown woman, a cousin of mine. When I went to the San Carlos Agency in 1885, I found her there. She was married and had six children. Her husband was a medicine man. She died shortly after I saw her, and all her children died afterward, and her husband died after I came back to McDowell. She was the only one of our three large families to get away.

I want to say something about the man who was married to my cousin. Her name was Cealiah (Worthless), and his was Jutahamaka (Swift Hawk). One time he was sick for a long time and no one could do him any good or cure him, so he was left to sleep one morning and finally given up for dead. The next morning everyone moved on to another camp, including his parents, and some men tore down the wigwam where he was lying and threw the sticks and thatch down on him as if he were dead. They piled on wood and the man's things and were about to light it when, to their surprise, they saw the man trying to crawl out of the pile. He asked them why they had put him there. All the men cried and told him that they had been sent to bury him, because he had died the day before. They said that he could not be alive, and someone called out his name, and he replied, "I am alive."

From that day on he told wonderful stories about what he saw in his death dreams. He said that while he was in that state he saw a cloud, and many women dressed in white and lots of children, and someone came up to him and told him to get up and walk away from that place, go home, and throw away all his clothes and put on new ones. Then he must heal people when they were nearly dead. He was advised how to sing over the sick and what songs would work best, and where he needed to put his hands or get someone to pierce the flesh so that he, the medicine man, could suck the bad blood out of the body, the bad blood that was killing the sick person.

That man Jutahamaka was dead from one morning to the next, and he was sick for a long time afterward. He was nothing but skin and bones. Well, sir, I have often witnessed when he would be called to see a sick person and would sing over them until some spirit came to point out the part of the body that was most in pain and poisoned, and then someone would take a sharp piece of glass and punch a hole there, and this man would suck out something like a worm or scorpion. He would take the thing from his mouth, mixed with blood, and hold it to the firelight and say that there were many more things like this in the body, and if he could get them all out the sick person would be well in a few days. It came true, sure enough; the man or woman would soon be up and acting like he or she was never sick. Sometimes, though, the sick person would die no matter how he sang. Even though he tried with all his power to bring spiritual aid, sometimes he failed, and at that point he would say that he did not have the power to help the sick and that he thought it best to find another medicine man or woman to do the job.

After they climbed out of the cave and got up onto the plateau, the soldiers and officers ordered the Apache scouts to go ahead with the Apache women and children captives, and not to let the Pimas or Maricopas near them. The Apache scouts were told to shoot if anyone disobeyed orders.

The whole command marched over the divide toward Four Peaks, and at the foothills they made a camp. The pack train and the horses

Four Peaks, at the southern end of the Mazatzal Mountains of Arizona. The peaks figure in the sacred geographies of many American Indian peoples of the region.

were left there, while the soldiers walked ahead. During the night three of the wounded captives died.

The next morning the command made an early start for Fort McDowell, and they arrived there toward evening. The remaining captives were put under guard in the horse corral.

There was a young lad among the captives whom Lieutenant E. D. Thomas took a liking to and chose to reward. This boy was my cousin, too. He had suffered a flesh wound, but it wasn't dangerous. His mother, a married sister, and, I think, two other children belonging to his family were all taken alive, but his father was killed. No grown men were taken alive at all.

This boy was given a room to share with me and two soldiers, a cook and, I think, one who used to take care of the officers' horses. The boy's name was Gaiamama, or Going By. We used to go down to the camp where the captives were held, and Gaiamama would go right over to his mother and sister and stay with them all day long. I would go home by myself or with some soldiers.

The captives were held at Fort McDowell for two weeks. One fine morning I missed Gaiamama and went down to the camp, but to my great surprise it was vacant. I came home so lonely, wondering what had happened to the people I talked to every day, what had become of them. Had the soldiers given them up to the demands of the Pimas and Maricopas, so that the innocent women and children would be butchered up the way they had killed all the rest of their people in that cave? There was no way I could find out what had happened to my aunt and her children, because I was not able then to speak English or Spanish and so was at a loss to learn a thing about the captives and my cousin Gaiamama.

The soldiers kept me at McDowell for about three weeks. Then they moved away from McDowell one morning with some Apache scouts, following the Verde River, and then they crossed the Salt River just above the present site of the Salt River Dam and camped. To my surprise, an Indian woman came in. The Apache scouts had come across a party of hostile Indians, and most all of them had gotten away, but they did overtake a woman who had a baby strapped to her back. The woman told me that she was my cousin, and she said that the party had been on their way to join the rest of our people at the cave. If they had arrived a little bit sooner, they would have all been killed, but the Salt River happened to be high and they had to wait to cross it. They had been camping along the banks, gathering greens and seeds to eat, for in wintertime plants grow there that the Apaches used to collect.

This woman cousin of mine told me that they knew that enemies had killed almost everyone in the cave, and the party, which had come down out of the upper Superstition Mountains, had stayed in a camp at a box canyon alongside the river. They sent a young man over to the cave, and he came back and told them of the great horrors he had seen, with a large cave that was full of dead men, women, and children. The party gave up on the notion of going across the river and moved south, trying to avoid soldiers and Pimas. Most of the older men thought that the soldiers would go home after having killed so many people, and so the women were moving freely along the riverside doing their gathering. Before they knew it, the scouts came up on them. The women who had no children ran away, but my cousin couldn't run fast enough and was taken prisoner. Some of the

Apaches hollered at the others to stop, but they only ran faster into the hills and got away.

My cousin said that there was a large camp at the eastern end of the Superstition Mountains, and that she and the others had been planning to go there and then go to Fort Grant on the San Pedro River to give themselves up. These Indians used to roam the Superstition and Pinal Mountains, but they are part of our people, too. Now they had to be on the lookout for soldiers, whom the Apache scouts guided into places they could not enter before, leading them through the country to waterholes.

The soldiers followed these scouts like they were blindfolded. The soldiers would never have seen an Indian camp if it hadn't been for the Apache Indian scouts, who went out and hunted for footprints. They knew every waterhole and every stream of running water.

The next morning the command moved camp, following a big wash upstream toward the Superstition Mountains near the Gold Field. We camped at a little spring where our people got water. The next day we came to the Salt River again. The following morning I sensed that there had been some trouble, and one of the scouts told me that the woman who had a child on her back had left the camp. He asked me whether she had said anything about where she was going. I told him no. I told him I was sorry for her, for she was my cousin, and besides I thought that she would be there to comfort me, since I was lonely and the only one left of a large tribe of Indians. He said that she was gone and no one knew where to hunt her.

The soldiers followed the Indian scouts as usual and camped at another spring. The next day the scouts came across some signs of Indians at the other end of the Superstition Mountains, so the soldiers marched that way and made camp on a little creek late in the evening. In a little while they moved again, and Captain Burns gave me something to carry—I suppose now it must have been bread, coffee, and sugar, things I did not know then. We went on a little way until we had to climb a big rough hill, and we got to the top at midnight all tired out. We found a mescal kiln built only a few days before. The mescal had been taken out, and there was waste scattered about. I ate all that I could find, and the soldiers seem to have liked it, too.

Toward morning the Apache scouts came creeping up the hill to tell the soldiers where the Indian camp was. It was nearly daybreak, and the officers were told to get the men ready for action. Some companies were already descending the hill, the scouts in the lead, and the rest of the command following. Near sunup they encircled several tepees, but there was nobody inside. The inhabitants must have seen the soldiers approaching from a long way off and run away. We noticed that there were trails in the rough rocks that led into the Superstition Mountains, and the tracks looked as if they had been made two or three days earlier. There was no point in following the trail, and no way to return home except around the big mountain, where we came in sight of the pack train and horses that we had left behind.

The next morning the soldiers and the rest of the command broke camp and climbed the hill again, going north this time. They entered the Pinal Mountains behind where Silver King is now. At that place the Pimas had massacred many Apaches, and we camped there. The next morning we went down to Sycamore Creek. The Apache scouts said that they had seen a camp about five miles from there, and the soldiers got ready to make a night march, taking plenty of rations and blankets. They had learned from experience to take those things, for they had suffered on long night marches before. They went a little way, then rested, then moved again and rested again, waiting for the scouts to return.

It was getting near morning. The soldiers were moving around busily, making for a certain place. I peeped over a hill and noticed a couple of small fires burning. The Apache scouts were there, calling for the people in the camp not to run away lest the soldiers shoot them. There were about five or six young men who did not heed the warning. They started to run into the bushes, and three were shot down immediately. All the soldiers and scouts rushed into the camp, ordering the people there to lower their weapons. The Apache scouts told them to come out and surrender so that they could be saved. But a few men came out and shot at the soldiers, and two soldiers and a couple of Indian scouts fell. The surprised soldiers scattered into the little hills, and then they started pouring in volleys from all directions.

After the sun came up the shooting ceased. The soldiers and scouts swamped the camp and found the wigwams riddled to pieces, and the inhabitants too. A few had hidden inside a deep hole made by water, and they came out and surrendered. Three were wounded, two so badly that they could not stand up and were left there to die. One of them was a fine-looking young man, shot through the bowels, his entrails hanging out.

3

The scouts scattered to see if they could find enemies or game. Some were to travel through the hills, then come in and make a report to the commanders. At this point, Lieutenant Schuyler and Al Sieber were in charge.

One evening two young men came in after they had looked the country over, and they brought with them some venison. They were taken to the commander and were disarmed and put under guard, for they had also brought in some cooked mescal, and this they got at an Indian camp, where they had warned the people to move in another direction, for some of the young men's near-relatives were in that camp. They had heard that their people had been massacred in a cave on the Salt River, and that soldiers were about and had enlisted lots of other Indians to find the remaining bands of Delshe's tribe.

Somehow Schuyler and Sieber, the chief of scouts, found out that the two young men had told the hostiles to make haste and keep out of the way of the soldiers. So they were kept under guard all the way to Fort Grant. One of the other scouts got mad, mad enough to shoot someone, and he went to the officers and told them that they were not treating the young men right, and if they cared to take all the scouts' weapons they should do so, and not just the weapons of those two simple-hearted young men. When he came back, he said that Schuyler and Sieber didn't say anything when he was talking to them so heatedly; he said they didn't pay any attention to him at all. But shortly thereafter some soldiers came to him and demanded his pistol, and he thought it best to quiet down and give them not only his pistol, but his rifle too. He was still mad, so he took the pistol from his belt and threw it, and then he took his gun and threw it a long way from the soldiers. The soldiers gathered them up and went off for the night. The next day the scout went off with the rest all the way to Fort Grant. The scouts didn't like the way he and the two young men had been treated. When they got to Fort Grant, they were all put in the guardhouse for two months.

The soldiers went off to be stationed in different places. Six companies were to be stationed at the San Carlos Agency until all the Apaches had settled down in the valley, and then the soldiers were to be sent away to other posts. Almost all the soldiers at Fort Grant left one morning, following Aravaipa Creek, and camped at an old ruin that looks as if, at one time, civilized people used to live there; there were many dugout houses, and the Indians might have chased them away and killed all the inhabitants. The next day the command camped at the upper end, at what is known as Hog Canyon. They had marched only about fifteen miles.

I heard afterward that a renegade Chiricahua Apache came into the camp and was told to give up his gun. He turned it to shoot the officers but was caught from behind, and his gun was taken from him. The next morning the soldiers marched him down the canyon and hanged him on a tree, where they left him to die.

The whole command crossed the Gila River and camped at the San Carlos Agency. A few days afterward Captain Burns's and Captain Price's companies were ordered to move downriver about five miles. The commanders were ordered to be on the lookout for hostiles, since the soldiers were right in the midst of the thickest of all kinds of Apaches now. The chiefs were Eskiminzin, Captain Chicatto, and Eskinaspas. They were the chiefs of the Aravaipa, Pinal, and San Carlos Apaches, who are different from the White Mountain, Coyote, and Chiricahua Apaches.

The two companies went downriver, and it was two weeks before they came back up again. There were about six or seven hundred Indians there, and they spent their time gambling, in which they bet all kinds of things except money, since they didn't know the value of money, only things. They gambled for clothing, or a horse or a saddle. A lot of people gathered around to watch the gamblers play.

Once a fellow won everything another fellow had, and the loser wouldn't give up any of the things that the other had won from him. He went off home and came back with a gun in his hand. The others who were standing there began to laugh at him, and in his rage he shot right into the crowd, not caring who he hit. He shot, and two men dropped dead. One of the men had a son in the crowd, and he began to fire back at the man who had killed his father. The other man ran away when he saw that he had killed two men, but the young man followed him and shot him at last. The whole camp was involved in the affair, and soldiers were called in to quiet down the trouble. The Indians gave up the troublesome parties to the soldiers, and they were held under guard.

Years afterward, the killing still hadn't been forgotten, and then another killing occurred. An Indian man killed a chief, and then he was killed in turn by the Apache Kid, because the chief was his uncle and stepfather. But it turns out that the chief was the son who killed the gambler all those years before, and the man who killed him was the gambler's son.

The Apache Kid became a renegade by taking up arms for his uncle. At the time he was the first sergeant of the Indian Company stationed there, charged with keeping order on the reservation. He thought that he was doing his duty as a US Scout by killing the man who had killed his uncle. He thought the agent and the chief of scouts might have given him credit for doing his job well. But the officers ordered that he and his followers be disarmed and locked up. He had been told to capture or kill anyone he saw shooting or killing another person.

Still, he was ordered to be disarmed and locked up without a fair trial. When he came in to the agency, Captain Pierce and Al Sieber told him and his men to go to the guardhouse. Sieber had already disarmed some of the men, but the Kid had not given up his gun. He made signs to the others to retrieve their gunbelts, which were piled up on a chair, and told them to get their guns while they were at it. Al Sieber must have heard him say this to his men, for he rushed to his tent to get his Winchester. Right behind him was Captain Pierce, who was the acting agent at the San Carlos Agency. He stepped through the door and jumped to one side just as a shot was fired. If he hadn't jumped, he would have taken the bullet straight through his shoulder, and it might have been fatal. I saw the shooting, for I was standing in a corner of Al Sieber's tent. When the shooting began I ran out as fast as I could and jumped into a gulch and went down to the slaughterhouse.

And so the Apache Kid became an outlaw. This was in the middle of June 1887.

The man he killed must have had it in his heart since childhood to get even someday. So he did, and he thought the matter settled forever, but instead he made the Apache Kid become as he was. In the end, public considerations will agree with the Apache Kid: from the start he did not unlawfully kill the man, and while the man was running away a whole group of scouts was shooting at him. But the Apache Kid got the whole blame, and afterward he was chased high and low, hiding from being seen, and those he might have killed tried to kill him first.

4

I must now go back to the time of the founding of the San Carlos Agency. There were no houses, only tents, and a large corral made of canvas, where rations were issued to the Indians. There were many different bands of Apaches there, and some were still slowly coming down to settle on the bottomland and had to draw rations. After Captain Burns and Captain Price settled the troubles, they went down to their camp, close to the river.

Often Indians came there who knew me. Some were related to me. They asked me to steal ammunition for them, but I told them I couldn't get it any more than they could, because the soldiers wouldn't trust me with any and would know that I would just give it away to the hostiles. I had no ammunition of my own to give them, and I told them that it was best just not to ask me. They replied that I should run away from the camp, and that they would take me so far away that the soldiers would never know where to look for me.

I was so bold as to answer that I had no near relatives living nearby, nobody I was anxious to see. But more Indians came around and insisted that I ought to leave, saying that a lonely cousin of mine had been crying because I was in the soldiers' camp. When I reached their camp, they said, then we would all move back toward the Superstition Mountains and Four Peaks, back to our old tramping grounds. I told them that they ought to know that I had no father, no mother, no aunt, no uncle, and that my little brother and my baby sister, whom I loved so much, had been killed; there were no living beings for me to be with after reaching the country where my people used to live.

A few weeks later the soldiers were ordered to move up to a camp headed by Eskiminzin and Captain Chicatto at Aravaipa Canyon. A few families of Pinal and Apache Mojaves were there. The soldiers went to the mountains and found an Indian camp, and they made their own camp within half a mile of it. They stayed there nearly two months. Again, every day, Indians came and talked with me, and they urged me to leave the soldiers. Some said that the soldiers were going to sell me off to the Pimas, and some said that the soldiers were going to kill me.

Clearly it was time for me to join them. So one night I left the camp. I always slept with Captain Burns, who made me lie next to the wall of the tent so that he would be in front of me. But no one noticed that I loosened the tent pegs right behind where I lay. About midnight the whole camp was quiet, and Captain Burns was sound asleep. I had gotten a blanket to use as a pillow, and I stuck it through one of the tent corners and then quietly moved under it. I stepped out into the darkness and ran off to the nearest Apache camp, listening at the door to see what people they were. I passed several camps until I came to one where I could clearly understand every word that was spoken by the people inside, but I also knew that these were not the people I was looking for. The man I was looking for was named Matawaha, Wind, who was my cousin. He lived with us until my mother was killed; then he went off and got married and lived among the Indians in the Pinal Mountains. He was the one who begged me to leave the soldiers' camp to come to his place, and the next day, he said, he would take me away up to the top of a mountain to hide until nightfall.

At last I came to Wind's tepee. It wasn't much of a tepee, because it was just hastily thrown together. My cousin took me to the chief, who was another cousin of mine, but the chief was afraid of the other Apaches, who were more numerous than the Pinal Apaches. So, he said, if the other Apaches gave him away for hiding a captive from the soldiers, then the chief would be liable to be put to death. He thought it best for me to go back to the soldiers' camp and stay with them for as long as I could, for there was no use coming back to the Indians again, since I had no close relations left.

Everyone cried while the chief talked, but they agreed with him. I cried, too, and went away. I made up my mind not to listen to any foolish advice ever again. When I reached Captain Burns's tent, I listened carefully and heard him snoring loudly. I crept in the same way I had left, and I quietly lay there.

The next morning I was scared of being whipped for staying out all night, but by good luck no one knew that I was ever gone. The sol-

The Verde Valley of central Arizona, at the heart of the Yavapai world.

diers returned to the main camp, where spring was beginning and the grass and cottonwood trees were green, and there were wildflowers everywhere.

The commander of F Company, Captain Price, was ordered to join the other commands near the agency. This must have been in 1873. G Company under Captain Burns, along with some Tonto Apache scouts who came to join them, went off one day to the northwest. Their first camp was at a spring called Coyote Hole. The next camp was below what is now the mining city of Globe. And the next camp was on the beginning of the Salt River, near the present site of the great Roosevelt Lake. We followed the lake down to Tonto Creek, and in its valley we saw a herd of wild horses. The Apache scouts shot at them, but I never learned whether they killed any or not.

I do not know how many days we traveled, passing the country where Payson and Strawberry are now. I remember, though, that a packer named Black Jack Long once shot about ten wild turkeys for the command.

Finally we came to Camp Verde and the Verde Valley. At this post there were just a few soldiers, for most of the command was out scouting. Captain Burns stayed only two days, then marched off to the west, passed through Cherry Creek, and came to a stone corral where US Mail riders stayed overnight. The next day we moved over the rolling fine grazing country that is now called Lonesome Valley. On the way the soldiers stopped to shoot at antelope, and the horse I was riding took fright and bolted. I held on tight, but the horse fell on its back, pinning me underneath. Only my leg was hurt.

That afternoon, the company, under Captain James Burns and Lieutenant E. D. Thomas, arrived at Fort Whipple. They remained there for several days. One day the soldiers were paid off. While we were at the San Carlos Agency they made me a soldier suit to wear, and I was dressed as tidy as any soldier and had learned the soldiers' ways, so that I saluted whenever I met an officer. When all the soldiers got their pay, the company bugler took me to a room where several officers were sitting. I walked into the room, head up, and stood so straight, hands on each side of my body, and so still that the officers began to laugh. I stood there and did not move, and they handed me some money. I did not know then how much money it was, but a couple of years later one of the soldiers told me that it was $1.45. I don't know what I did with the money, since I didn't know its value in those days. I know it now, and I wish I had been around at the place called Battle Flat, between Crown King and Prescott, when some Apache Indians captured some money. They cut the paper money up to make cigarette paper, and they threw away all the coins because they were so heavy and they were traveling on foot.

Well, after the soldiers got their money, they marched away, climbing the big pine mountain that stands off to the west of Prescott and down to Skull Valley. They camped there. That evening Captain Burns handed me a piece of white paper, and also some green paper, and pointed me toward a house a little way off from the camp. I ran off to the house and gave the papers to a man I saw there. He went off in quick order and came back with some eggs. I went running off to camp with them. I noticed that both officers were laughing, but after a while Captain Burns began talking and reached for a stick. All at once he came at me and hit me on my back, swearing and hitting me as I danced around, crying. But after a while the man to whom I had given the money came running up to Captain Burns and handed him something, and they began talking and laughing, too. Then Captain Burns threw away the stick. He must have given me a five- or ten-dollar bill and expected me to wait for the change. But he should have known better than that, because I was not civilized enough to know the value of different kinds of money, nor would I have known how much an egg is worth, whether a dollar or five dollars or five cents. I did not know how to buy anything in those days, nor would I have known how to ask to buy something. It seems to me that it was foolish on Captain Burns's part to punish me for doing what I did. I was willing to do anything he asked, as much as I was able to understand him.

He might have been right, though, since he was starting to teach me how to be mindful about doing business with people.

5

The next day, at noon, we arrived at Date Creek. There I stayed, doing all kinds of chores as if I were a member of the family, such as herding chickens for Mrs. Thomas. Every day the chickens would scatter away from the house and hide in the brush, and every day I would gather them.

In the summer of 1873, Captain James Burns went off to the desert country, toward Fort Mojave. He commanded G Company of the Fifth US Cavalry. Why he went to the desert I do not know. This time he didn't take me with him. The officer who had given me the name Mikey, Lieutenant E. D. Thomas, had a wife and two children, and I suppose that Captain Burns asked Mrs. Thomas to care for me while he was gone. I had hard jobs, like looking after the chickens and fetching water. The water at Date Creek had to be hauled in by wagon from the creek itself, which was about a mile away. Soldiers who were in jail for something would do this work, bringing in two or three barrels at a time, and when the water wagon came I would run over the hills to fill up little cans with water and take them out to the chickens.

Over by the creek there was an Indian camp, and I could talk to the people there, because they spoke the same language as our people. They were what were called Apache Yumas. There were lots of little boys and girls among them, and I used to go there when Mrs. Thomas was at home and play with them. Some of the old men made me a small bow and some arrows so that I could shoot at targets with the other children. I got used to staying around that camp almost all day long, and when Mrs. Thomas wanted me she sometimes couldn't find me, so she would have soldiers hunt for me. They would find me at the Indian camp and rush me back to the fort.

The Indians often asked me about where I came from and how I happened to be with the soldiers. I would tell them that my people used to live near Four Peaks, or Weegajochehaw, "the mountain that has been chopped up." I did not tell them that all my people had been killed at the cave, because remembering would always make me cry. I never felt happy.

Some other Indians came in from the west with their chief, Najawalawale'lah, Tall Black Fellow. Captain Burns and Lieutenant Thomas had been out in the desert for going on a month. One day, while out gathering up the chickens scattered over the hills, I saw a whole column of men, some mounted on horses, some marching in rows of four and five men, coming over the hills. They were about seven and a half miles away. I was frightened and ran home, forgetting all about the chickens, and tried to tell the news to Mrs. Thomas. I made some motions, pointing toward the hills, and said, "Indians! Indians!" Mrs. Thomas thought that some hostiles must be coming to jump the garrison, which was made up of just a few soldiers who had been left behind, and she and I went over to their quarters. I suppose she told the soldiers what I had said about the Indians coming, for they got their guns and ran off. Then one of the soldiers came back over and said that it was Captain Burns and Lieutenant Thomas, coming in with lots of Indians.

After that time I spent time with still more Indian children. Captain Burns and Lieutenant Thomas had not had any trouble rounding up the Indians, who were also Apache Yumas.

The soldiers used to come down to the camp and bring the Indians up to their fort. I always went along to see what would happen. Once I went along with some soldiers down to the corral. I saw that the soldiers had taken the windows off their quarters and had all put on cartridge belts. They all had guns. I went on to the gathering. There was a narrow strip of land between the soldiers' quarters and the corral, and this was where the Indians gathered. I noticed a great tall Indian with hair down to his rump and a pistol strapped to his belt. He said, "I'm ready for anything, whatever happens. I was told to give myself up to the soldiers and be saved."

I stood there listening to what that Indian was saying to his followers until Captain Burns took me away from there. I had to go out to an underground place where I found Mrs. Thomas and several other women and children. The officers had been looking out for trouble, and they sent their wives and children underground before the shoot-

Apaches attending a camp revival at the San Carlos Agency in 1921.
Mike Burns lived at the agency two generations earlier.

ing started. They expected a great shootout at any minute. Because I
had been with the Indians, I hadn't heard anything about it.

Word had come down from Fort Whipple ordering Captain Burns
to gather the Indians near Camp Date Creek and to capture their
leaders, clap them in irons, and chain them to each other.

Some of the Indians had been in parties that had been seen near
the country around Gila Crossing. They had killed several men and
driven off some livestock, and their trail led to where the other Apache
Yumas had gathered down near the Harquahala country. None of
those Indians knew anything about the killings. But Captain Burns
was ordered to have the guilty Indians pointed out to him and bring
them to Fort Whipple and the guardhouse. Without knowing for
sure whether they did the killings, Captain Burns took six headmen
off to Fort Whipple, where they were kept under guard. I saw them
afterward; they were in chains, with big round iron balls tied to their
chains, and they had to carry these on their backs.

After the six headmen were put under guard, the rest of the Indians
went back to their camp. Many slipped away that night, but the rest
stayed. A few days later the soldiers took the Indians toward Prescott,
then down to the Verde River, where they joined many other bands of
Apaches. For several months afterward the Indians who had escaped

from Date Creek came back willingly and gave themselves up to the soldiers. They were disarmed at once. The men were put in the guard-house, while the women and children went back to the old camp. Later, they also were taken down to the Verde River and settled along the valley. They were fed flour, sugar, coffee, and fresh beef every day, as long as they agreed to stay there and not fight against the soldiers or other Indians.

There was a white man living on the Agua Fria River near the confluence of Ash Creek. His name was Townsend. He was part Indian, of either the Cherokee or Creek nation; no one knew exactly what he was or the truth of his pedigree. He was a terror on the Apache nation. Many Indians say that when he went out to the hills he always had two big bloodhounds and a fast horse; he had a spyglass and a Winchester rifle and two pistols, and he did lots of killing. He would follow the Indians' trails to their camps, using his dogs, and then dash in and kill them while they were asleep. He would keep on shooting whenever he saw an Indian, and kill all the inhabitants, and set fire to the camp so that the Indians would burn up in their tepees, the old people and the children turned into ashes. The men would be out raiding or hunting and return home to find their wives, fathers, mothers, and children among the ruins.

No Indian was daring enough to kill Townsend for a long time, because they had no firearms to match his.

Townsend had some corn planted at his place, and the Indians would go there when it ripened, posting the women to keep watch, because Townsend would roam the country looking for traveling Indians. Sometimes they would see him out in the field, and then they would wait until nightfall and crawl out to get some corn, and then make for their homes, safe. But other times, Townsend would stay in the field, waiting for Indians to show up. He had fixed wire down near the ground around the cornfield, so that when he fired shots at the Indians they would start to run through the field and get tangled up in a bunch. That made a good target for him, and he would shoot several at a time that way.

After a while there weren't many Indians left to undertake to steal his corn. But Townsend's ranch was the only one that had any corn around there at the time, though it was more expensive than what it is nowadays, since it cost many Indians their lives for just a few ears.

Townsend killed more Indians, I guess, than any single man in the West. He went out into the country with his two bloodhounds just to shoot Indians, and he would often bring their heads home with him, or sometimes cut notches into his house or a nearby cottonwood tree to record how many he killed.

I once heard that he boasted to some old-timers that he had killed ninety-eight Indians. Others said it was a hundred and fifteen. If there was doubt about it, he could just point to his house and that tree.

Because of his killing, he made many enemies among the Indians, and innocent people paid for it. The Indians wanted vengeance, but they couldn't get Townsend himself, so they thought that maybe the other whites had put him there to kill Indians. So in this way they decided that they should kill whites, or else they would just steal livestock—horses and cattle, but not sheep or goats, since these tasted somewhat strong, different from venison or beef or horsemeat.

At last Townsend was killed, sometime in the fall of 1873, or maybe 1874. Now, General Crook wanted all the Indians in the countryside to come to Camp Verde and to stay there in peace, where they would be given rations and clothing and protected by the soldiers. Word reached him that there were still some families holding out in the Bradshaw Mountains. There were about fifty enlisted Indian scouts stationed at the post, and Crook sent one of them with a note to show any soldiers or strangers he encountered that he was on an official errand for the government. This Indian mounted a pony and left Camp Verde. He went up Copper Canyon, then down Ash Creek, and crossed the Agua Fria River and Big Bug Creek, going a little west of what is now Cordes Station. Townsend got him in his sights somewhere around there, for when the Indian crossed a gulch and started going up a little uphill grade, he noticed a man on a horse coming along behind him about a mile away. He thought that another Indian had been sent to keep him company, and at any rate his pony was getting tired out. He was going along slowly uphill when a shot rang out. His horse dropped dead, and he was hit in the leg.

The scout saw that the rider was flanking him toward a little hill with a cedar tree that looked down on where he was lying. He also saw that there was a little brushy gulch near where he and his horse lay, so he crawled into it and waited for a few minutes. He saw a gun pointing out from behind the cedar tree at his dead horse, and then just the very top of a hat. Just at that moment he decided to shoot through the little cedar tree, knowing that if he missed he would be dead. But he thought he could hold off for at least a while, for he had an old Henry rifle, the kind that used to be given to scouts, with seven or eight .44 caliber rounds in the magazine and muzzle. He fired at the tree, and he saw no more of that moving object. He stayed in his place for a long while, until the sun went over the hills, and then quietly crawled up the gulch to where he could look down at the cedar tree. It was a good distance away, but he was afraid that the man might come out and shoot, so he didn't dare straighten up.

He went up over the hill and down to Dripping Spring, where he drank some cold water. He stayed there all night. The next morning he could barely raise himself up on his one good leg, but he got up and found a stick to use as a cane, and then, going very slowly, went down to where Turkey Station is now, up the canyon and a little east of the Middleton Mine, on the rough side of the mountains. At last an Indian from the camp met him. His leg was getting swollen, and he was making no headway. The man who met him was called Arahadgalitsaw, One Enemy, and the scout was called Meenetgaboda, The End of a Boat.

The next day the scout told of his encounter, saying that he had been sent to bring the Indians down to Camp Verde lest soldiers swarm all over their homes and hunt them down. It was going on four days since he had had his fight, and he believed that there was a chance he had killed his pursuer.

When the word got out, most of the Indians refused to believe that it could have been Townsend. He was a hard man to see and shoot at, they said. He always had big dogs, but there were no dogs there. The Indians said that the scout must have shot some other white man. But he told them to go look, and he directed them to where the dead horse lay, and said that they should look for a single cedar. A party went off and found the scene, and to their great surprise they found a grave, and inside it the right man, the one they had been hoping to kill for so long. Soldiers must have come along and buried the body. The Indians took it out so that the coyotes could have their fun and have a feast on him.

I found out afterward that Lieutenant Thomas had taken a detachment of G Company to Dripping Spring and found Townsend. A single bullet had gone under his shoulder and come out the other, and it must have passed right through his heart.

From the time Townsend was killed, there was no other killing done by Indians and whites. That goes to show that all the troubles rose from what he had done. It looks hard for his remaining family, but these are the facts. There are men and women alive today who can remember and tell stories about how Townsend used to kill Indians just so he could be known as a great Indian fighter of the Wild West.

Townsend's death was hard on his family. I know three of his boys, and I understand there was a girl, too. The oldest, Ben Townsend, was well known as a miner at McCabe Chaparral. Chauncey Townsend was a miner and cowboy around Humboldt and Mayer. The other boy, also around McCabe, I never met or knew much about. I often heard them say that their father was ambushed by Apaches around Dripping Spring, which we called Quealtugoowaw, "a red rock bank where the water drips over it."

I tried to make them forget about what had happened to their father, because the man who killed Townsend is dead now. But Townsend would have finished his work had the Indian scout not had a gun, but just a bow and arrow. Meenetgaboda shot him from a distance of two hundred yards. If he hadn't, the Indian would never have seen another day, and Townsend would have had another head to add to his trophies, and he would have gone on to do more killing.

6

One time a party of Indians went to a camp out on the Agua Fria River, near the foothills of Copper Mountain a little east of Mayer. There were some soldiers there. The Indians were hunting rabbits, which were plentiful down on the flats between the river and Ash Creek. One group of Indians came upon the soldiers' camp, and the soldiers shot two of them and took the rest under guard. One Indian ran for a way down toward the river, but when he reached the side of the hill he was shot dead. The other group of Indians saw what was happening to their friends, and they ran off and crossed the Agua Fria River and Ash Creek too, and went down to their main camp near the Ball Mountains, just beyond the Squaw Peaks down by Camp Verde. After the whole tribe found out what had happened, they called a war council, and some runners went across the Verde River to call on the Tontos for help. Others went off to where Jerome is now, to tell them to come help clean out the white newcomers who had been killing their people without provocation. Many answered the call.

A few days later the warriors set out toward the soldiers' camp. They found that the soldiers had gone, making their way to Fort Whipple. They went off to look along the roads that passed through the countryside, full of pack trains and wagons carrying grub out to the new mining camp below Prescott. The warriors crossed the Agua Fria where the Humboldt smelter is now, and they climbed up to the top of the hill. There they saw at a distance six mounted men, and about twenty-five or thirty mules loaded with something. Two men rode ahead, and four behind.

A deep gulch lies there, just below McCabe. The Indians decided to go down into the gulch and wait there for the six men and their pack mules. The chiefs were Navchucavir, whose name means "running a race with the sun," and Echamawahu, whose name means "enemy head." These two sat right in the gulch, only a few feet from the road, where the water rushed up against some dirt and large flat rocks. Several men raised these rocks to make a kind of breastwork, and others were posted on a little hill to watch for the approaching train. They called down and said that the men were almost there, and at last the hooves of the animals could be heard. Many of the Indians were uneasy, but the chiefs said they could run if they wanted to, but that they weren't going to move.

The two forward riders came into the gulch. The Indians did not want them. They waited for the other four, and then shot at them. Three dropped from their horses, but the other one turned around and started chasing the Indians with the two forward riders at his side. At last one fell dead, so that there were just two of them left. They fought bravely, and one Indian, the brother of chief Navchucavir, was killed. The two white men backed their way over the hill, and one was seen dragging his gun. The chiefs said to wait, because the white men could have been waiting on the other side of the hill to pick the Indians off, like shooting at birds in the trees. Some of the Indians were mad because one of their best men had been shot, but they weren't satisfied at killing only four white men.

They debated for a while, some saying that they should get the other white men, who were probably out of ammunition, and others saying that they shouldn't follow them, but instead gather up the animals and drive them off to the old camp. That's what they did, and the Indians had horses and plenty of mule meat to last for several days.

Men had been posted as lookouts around the camp, and they reported that there was no enemy in sight. But after four days, soldiers came unnoticed and fired right into the camp while the Indians were playing a game like ring toss, gambling for things that had been captured. The soldiers had hidden in a cedar flat, and when they fired some of the Indians fell, while others ran to get their guns. There was a deep gulch outside the camp, and the soldiers had to cross it, which took a while. So most of the people were able to escape into the mountains.

There was also a high hill outside the camp, and the warriors under chief Navchucavir decided to make their stand there. The soldiers were just about to set fire to the camp when the Indians starting firing down volleys at them.

There was great confusion among the soldiers, who tried to get out of the way of the shots. They ran back into the gulch that they had just crossed, but the Indians kept firing. The soldiers ran back into the cedar flat and kept on going. When the Indians came back to the camp they found that four of their people had been killed: an old man and his son, and a couple of old women, along with two Tontos, a woman and a child. So that made six in all. The Indians looked on the ground and saw that there was a lot of blood where the soldiers had been standing, which showed that many of them had been shot, but they must have carried off the dead and wounded. Some of the young men followed the soldiers' trail and found three dead horses; they kept on following, and found bloodstains all along the way.

The Indians decided to move their camp toward Waulkayauayau, "pine tableland," which is what they called the Black Hills behind Jerome. Navchucavir was going to kill all the animals on the battleground, for he was very angry about his brother's death. But his fellows persuaded him not to act foolishly, because he was respected as a leader and had to act like one. Too, the animals had to be saved to carry them up to the mountains before more soldiers came and overtook them. A man who had been wounded was put on a horse and taken up into the hills, with the stock following him at a fast gait.

The man recovered from his wound, but three years later Hualapais killed him up near the Grand Canyon. He had a good horse, and he took it to a Hualapai settlement to trade it for a gun. There had been some trouble between the Apache Mojaves and the Hualapais, and many Hualapais had been slaughtered. This lone man came into the Hualapai camp. He had no idea that he would be treated badly, but he was killed as he sat and told them about events. One of them was a treaty that his people were about to make with the whites—but then the whites came in and killed several Indians, so they rejected the treaty and kept in the hills out of the enemy's sight.

Some long time afterward, a Hualapai family came into an Apache Yuma camp down beyond Kirkland, near the desert. The old man among them took sick, and he said that the women in the camp were trying to kill him. The Hualapai man got worse and worse and blamed it on almost everyone in the camp, and he said that if he were able he would shoot everybody. He wasn't strong enough to get up to get his bow and arrow. Still, the other Hualapais began to worry that the Apache Yumas were getting tired of his threats, and they asked him to stop talking about not feeling well.

A few weeks passed, and then a young man whose relatives had been killed by Hualapais turned around and killed the youngest of the family, and then an old woman, and then the old man who was just lying there sick. He killed all three of them, just because the old man had been talking so much about what he would do when he got well enough to stand up.

The news quickly got around about what the young man had done.

Soon there was a big fight near Prescott. The Yavapais made a war council against the soldiers and anybody else they might come across, and they sent a party off to the Bowers Ranch to drive off some cattle. The party crossed Granite Creek about four miles below Fort Whipple, but some whites overtook it, killed two Indians, and drove the livestock back home.

Shortly afterward about a hundred Indians got together and crossed Lynx Creek, and someone said that the soldiers were coming up the gulch at a place called Eekisjava, "a pole sticking up," near a gap called Quathasiketta, "brown-looking painted rocks." The Indians went there, but they didn't have many guns. Still, most of the braves were willing to fight against any odds, so they crept up close to the road and hid behind some bear grass and burrobrush. They listened for the horses' hooves. Just when they were ready to attack, some timid fellows jumped out of their hiding places and ran out in sight of the soldiers. The soldiers were thus warned, but most of them ran anyway; only a few stood their ground. At that fight three Indians were killed, but when the soldiers retreated they left some horses on the ground for the Indians.

There was some disagreement among the Indians about that fight. Some believe that they would have killed all the soldiers if it hadn't been for the ones who jumped out of their hiding places and didn't shoot at the soldiers.

Before that battle took place, about two hundred Tonto Apaches crossed the Verde River near where the Arizona Power Company line now crosses it. They passed Government Spring and topped Government Gap, and there the advance scouts said that they saw many soldiers coming up the deep canyon. This is the headwater of Sycamore Creek, which empties into the Agua Fria River. It was getting late in the afternoon, and the Indians knew that the soldiers would soon make camp, even though they were deep in the canyon and the banks of rocks on each side were very steep. Echawamahu told the Indians to be careful not to let the soldiers see or hear them. When night came, the Indians could see the campfires of the soldiers very plainly. No one slept. At dawn the Indians crept up to the edge of the soldiers' camp. The soldiers were standing in rows getting ready for breakfast, and the Indians let loose volleys of gunfire. Soon nothing could be seen but dead soldiers and dead horses. The Indians got lots of guns and ammunition and fresh horses to ride, and horsemeat to eat and take home to their people.

On their way home the Tontos came to a Yavapai camp. They told the Yavapais to follow their trail back to the canyon, where they would find plenty of horsemeat. Some Yavapais went there, but the dead horses were spoiling and were not fit to eat. They gathered the bodies of the horses and soldiers and burned them up. They didn't bother to count how many soldiers had died, but there were a lot of them, and a lot of dead horses, too.

Many people have made inquiries about that fight and want to know just where it happened. I don't think there are any Indians now living who could show the place. I learned the facts about this from the old people, and they have died since. There were only two old men who used to talk about seeing the bodies of the soldiers, and all those dead horses.

The same Tontos made another raid. They went across the Bradshaw Mountains to the headwaters of the Hassayampa River and found cattle there. There were about fifteen Tontos, daring fellows. They drove the cattle back the same way they had come, and after crossing the Agua Fria River they supposed they were safe and made camp, and they all slept soundly, with no one on watch.

Early the next morning, a party of white men crept up to the Indians and shot them in the head while they were asleep. They cut the heads off, and so it is supposed that Townsend was in the gang, because all the Indians used to say that he always cut the heads off of the Indians he killed, and packed them home.

The Tontos lived in the country around the East Verde River, passing on beyond where Payson is now and down into the Sierra Ancha, and all through the valleys of the Tonto Basin, and across the ranges of the Mazatzal Mountains. They often met with Apache Mojaves and intermarried with them. Our people did the same, and for that reason most of these people are related to each other and came out together to fight enemies. And for that same reason, sometimes innocent people would be massacred for what other people had done.

7

There were two chiefs of the Mojave Indians living along the Colorado River. Their names were Nahtahdavbah and Ahsojithaw, and they were the first to lead white men up the Hassayampa River and on to the Agua Fria River, up the Black Canyon to its headwaters.

A party of white men under the leadership of someone who was called something like Bawoleuna met many Yavapai Indians at the site of what is now the great Humboldt smelter. Some of the Yavapais talked with Nahtahdavbah, and he told them that many white people would soon be coming into this country. He knew about white people. He came to speak English because when the first party of white men came up the Colorado River, the Yumas and Mojaves got together and killed many of them and threw the bodies into the water. A bigger party of white men came and surrounded the Indians. They captured twelve chiefs. The white men then killed all the other Indians except this Nahtahdavbah. They took him away and put him on a train, and he was sent back east for about ten years, and then brought back the way he was sent, by way of the railroad to San Francisco, and then by steamboat up to the Mojave settlements on the Colorado. When Nahtahdavbah went away, Ahsojithaw was named chief.

Nahtahdavbah came back, and he told the Indians he met about the buildings he had seen. He said that he had seen houses that stood so tall against the sky, and people walking up in those buildings with all their windows and doors, and iron wagons that crept along the ground, like living things, needing only water and fire, and when they approached the city they would holler like a squaw, and ring their bells when going through town. The machines breathed and smoked and pounded the ground.

There are still two or three very old Yavapais living today who remember his stories, and what Nahtahdavbah said was true, those things about buildings and locomotives.

When Nahtahdavbah went back down the Granite Mountains and toward the desert a couple of years later, he saw Bawoleuna and some white people along the Hassayampa River. At that time white men and Mexicans used to prospect for gold, picking it up on the ground near Congress Junction and Wickenburg and the upper parts of the Hassayampa. The Yumas and Mojaves used to work for the miners, carrying water and bringing wood to camp and cutting hay. They lived in harmony with the newcomers. This Bawoleuna was a good and just man, and it seems that he influenced others to stay on good terms with the Indians, because the Indians showed no hatred to the whites when they came into the country as long as they treated the Indians justly.

That wasn't the case along the river, where soldiers and settlers drove the Yumas from their homes. The Yumas came up into the Yavapai country and camped in the Bradshaw Mountains and Lonesome Valley. They stayed for about two years. Bawoleuna was friendlier than the other whites, and when he went to the Colorado the Indians returned there. He made a camp called La Paz near where Parker is now. The whites found gold without having to dig for it, there and up around Agua Caliente, and they remained friendly with the natives.

Still, some young Indians who worked around Camp Date Creek, cleaning and doing odd jobs, once went into a camp of strange white people, and the whites shot them down for no reason. And then more than a hundred men and women were slaughtered near Kirkland, a place that afterward was called Skull Valley. It was called that because when white settlers arrived, they found so many skulls and bones on the ground. The people were defenseless, and many were killed trying to run away.

Years before, a white man named Weaver, who used to live up at the headwaters of the Hassayampa, gave their chief, a man named Echawawchaconma (whose name means "hitting an enemy"), a piece of paper saying that he had never had any trouble with them and that nobody should. Weaver told the chief that he should show the paper to any white men who happened by—but first, that they should be sure to hide their weapons and leave their bows and arrows in the hills. That way they would not be molested.

Echawawchaconma's people were at a spring a few miles west of

Iron Springs, near where Prescott is now. Every time a white man
came by, Echawawchaconma would show him the paper, to prove
that he was a warm friend of the man who wrote it. As they were
traveling, Echawawchaconma's band came upon an army camp, and
he approached to show the soldiers the paper, followed by his people,
one by one. They came up to a tent where they supposed the commanding officer was, and Echawawchaconma went inside with the
paper. The officer inside pushed his hat back so that he could have
a clear view and aimed his gun. Echawawchaconma kept coming,
waving the paper, and the officer fired at him at such close range that
the chief's clothes caught on fire. The soldiers began to fire, shooting
at the Indians, some of whom ran through the camp to try to find
weapons, so that the soldiers must have killed some of their own men
while shooting at them.

Some of the Indians got away and went back to their camp. They
thought that they had lost their leader, for they had seen their chief
fall, on fire. But two days later Echawawchaconma came into camp.
The bullet went through his shoulder, but no bones were broken. He
was almost dead when he got there, and he died soon after.

This massacre took place without any provocation whatever.

Two Indians who worked for a white man named Lehi, the agent
to the Mojaves, were suspected of helping organize the massacre. One
was a Mojave and the other was a Yavapai. Some Indians killed Lehi,
and the other Indians planned to kill them, too, but some relatives of
the Yavapai man persuaded them to let it pass, saying that he was one
of those who had gone to the Colorado River a long time ago and had
been made to bring white people into the country.

A few months afterward, Nahtahdavbah and Ahsojithaw sent for
the headmen of the Apache Yumas to come down to the Colorado
for a peace council. About twenty-five Yumas came into the Mojave
camp. They were given clothing and food and told to make their camp
a short distance away. While they were asleep, someone attacked them
and killed two of their number. They blamed this on Nahtahdavbah
and Ahsojithaw.

Nahtahdavbah and Ahsojithaw then started killing and making
war against the whites, afterward making the whites believe that
someone else was responsible and that they were innocent of these

murderous deeds. They made their wars in secret, and then threw the bodies of the dead into the rivers so that they would not tell of their acts. Then they would go and tell false stories that the Apaches had committed the murders. The Oatman family, for instance, was destroyed by Mojaves. The Mojaves had come across the desert toward the Maricopa settlements, but they saw the Oatman camp and reckoned that they could get away with killing them without notice. So they did it. They took two or three children. One girl had her face tattooed and her hair dyed with mesquite pitch and mud. She eventually became Nahtahdavbah's wife.

Nahtahdavbah was scared once the country started to fill up with white people. He decided to fool the whites by giving the girl to a white family, saying that he had bought her from the Yavapais. He said that he had paid a lot for her but did not want anything in return except the whites' respect and trust. The Yumas and Mojaves didn't have anything to do with the murderous deeds, he insisted. Instead, he said, the mountain Indians were to blame.

At that point, none of the mountain Indians had met any whites. The Yumas, on the other hand, had been fighting with the whites on and off for a long time there on the Colorado River. You can see the breastworks at Fort Yuma where the soldiers fought the Indians. But then Nahtahdavbah came back, and he spoke English, and he convinced the whites to let his people keep their land and give them guns to fight the mountain Indians.

This was how the whites came to believe that the Apaches were a bad set of people, even though the Apaches had not seen them or done anything to warrant their hatred. The Apaches were blamed for things they did not do, and soon innocent men, women, and children were dying at the hands of the whites.

As these hostilities were just beginning, a single armed man came out to Camp Date Creek. I learned afterward that he was General Howard, sent by the Great Father in Washington to hold peace talks with Pakota, who was also called José Coffa or Coffee—General Grant called him José Pakota—and with a young man, his cousin, whose name was Tugodawa, which means "hanging on a limb," who afterward was called Washington Charlie. The two had just come from the western country, where the Yumas lived.

Pakota, a Kwevkepaya leader. He was also known as José Coffa, Coffee, and José Pakota.

General Howard asked the chiefs at Date Creek—Chawmah, Jacoma, Snook, Chamajyah, and Matgowoo—who would go with him to Washington. There was a great deal of talking back and forth. Some of the chiefs said that whoever went with the white man would never see home again. But Pakota agreed to go and represent the Apache Yumas, saying that there was nothing like going to see other countries and people. His cousin Tugodawa said he would go, too, and so did Chawmah, his half-Mojave nephew, who was always ready to be useful. The idea of leaving home forever scared the other chiefs. But Pakota was young and strong and willing to undertake any adventure, even if it cost him his life. The other two young men had the same attitude.

General Howard said that another white man would be detailed to go with them and take care of their needs. He was a doctor, as much as I can remember. His name was Dr. McNeil, or maybe Nailty. At any rate, he went with them. All this took place in late fall, about November, of 1870.

First they went to Skull Valley, then to Fort Whipple, where they stayed for three days and were outfitted with clothing. I was there. I traveled to Camp Verde with them. An Indian came into their camp and said he had heard that we were traveling east to see the Great Father in Washington. He said that some Yavapais had been imprisoned in Camp Verde. They had been locked up for three months after questioning whether their people would be safe if they came in from the hills. Pakota went to the commanding officer with Joe Gacka, the interpreter at Camp Verde, and showed him papers from General Howard showing that he had been summoned to Washington to see the Great Father and make peace throughout the land. Pakota secured the release of the Yavapais, telling them to bring their people into camp. The head chief, whose name was Mojave Charlie, said that he wanted to bring his people down from the mountains to live in the bottomlands and farm there. He wanted the Great Father's assurance of protection, because his people had done nothing wrong and wanted to live at peace.

There was a man there named Mr. Gentile, a traveling photographer, who had a boy who could speak Mojave. The boy had been captured by Pimas and brought to Florence after they had killed off all his people. This Indian's name was Wassaja, which means "motioning to come." Afterward he was called Carlos Montezuma, and he is now a doctor in Chicago.

This man Gentile arranged with General Howard to take us along. So we said good-bye to our Yavapai brothers and told them to be good people until we came back one day. We crossed the Mogollon Rim, then went to the Little Colorado and on to Fort Apache. We stayed there for a month. Then General Howard came up with three Pimas or Papagos and three Apaches whose fathers were the chiefs of the Aravaipa and the Coyoteros, who were the same as Chiricahuas. There was also one Mexican Apache interpreter. With the Pimas was a missionary whose name was Coke.

We moved away from there with General Howard and three great wagons loaded with stuff for us. Each wagon had about twenty-four mules and seats covered with a canvas top. General Howard, Dr. McNeil, and Mr. Coke had another wagon, and Mr. Gentile had his own outfit. We traveled north and then east for about seven days until we reached Albuquerque, New Mexico, where we found that the Rio Grande had risen. We had to stand on the bank and look at the city for three days before we could cross. Then came a crew of Mexicans with flatboats. We crossed with the light teams. Then the heavy wagons tried to cross, but the swollen river overturned the boats and swept the wagons and livestock away, and all our food and clothing along with them.

General Howard went around town and came back with a wagon loaded with clothing and grub. We traveled on for two days to Santa Fe, where we boarded a stage that traveled all day and all night. It took four days and four nights for us to get to a big city, which must have been Denver, Colorado. We stayed there for about fifteen days, and then at last a train came, and we were told to get on and sit down. The train pulled out. I don't know which direction we went, but I think we went north and east for two nights and three days.

Someone sang out "Chicago!"

There Mr. Gentile shook hands with us, and he and the boy and a relative of ours got off. Dr. McNeil also got off, saying that he had to go in another direction to New York City. That left General Howard and Mr. Coke to see us to Washington.

At last we arrived. We were there about two weeks before President Grant was ready to see us. One morning our old friend General Howard came in and told us to wash ourselves clean and get ready to go to the Capitol and have a talk with the President, the man who sent for us to come to him from so far away. So General Howard took us to the Capitol, and we did not know what to think when we saw the rows of soldiers standing in front of that huge building, their guns upward. We went up some steps, and there were more soldiers. After some more steps we were shown to a large room. There President Grant was seated. He rose, took our hands, and led us to our seats.

He was a short man, thickly built, with a short beard, and he told us that he had sent for us and wanted to tell us that peace must be with every living soul throughout America. As he conquered the Southern people and made them come to terms, he wanted the Indians to be peaceful, too. As long as they stayed on government land, he would see to it that the Indians were supported with food and clothing, and he also wanted the children to be sent to schools to be educated like white people. He wanted all of us present to take these words back to our people and to tell the Indians that the Great Father in Washington would take good care of those who obeyed and stayed on the reservation and farmed and raised something to eat for themselves and their families. No more staying out in the hills, because anyone who did not heed his words would be chased down and killed, for every bad man had to be punished. All those who heard him now were to help the government settle the warlike peoples, and the sooner they came to peace the better it would be for everyone.

President Grant said, "I want to elect all of you to be chiefs of your people. I am going to give each of you a likeness of myself, and a paper that shows that you were appointed by me at this place, Washington, the capital of America." He handed each of us a letter and a medal with his own likeness on it, and he told us to show it to anyone who doubted us.

The President also handed out notes to draw some money. General Howard took the Indians over to the paymaster, and each one was given fifty dollars. They did not know what to do with all that money, but the President said that they could stay and see all the things the white man had made, and even go to New York City to see the great buildings.

So we went to New York on a steamer along the coast of the Atlantic Ocean. We went to a place called Governor's Island that had a lot of great guns, one so big that a man could sit inside the barrel. We saw the sights of New York and then boarded a train, reaching a place that I took to be Philadelphia, then traveling down to New Orleans for several days. There I saw many ships and steamers coming and going. One of them took us back to Washington, where the President gave us more papers to read to our people when we reached home. We got on a train again and came to Chicago, where we stayed for a few days and met our old friend Dr. McNeil. From Chicago it took four nights and five days to reach San Francisco, and there we were shown many places: we saw where the coins were made and went to the lake and again saw great steamers going in and out. Dr. McNeil, Mr. Coke, and the three Pimas were still with us, and we were told to get ready to go on a steamer to the Gulf of California, where another smaller steamer would take us to Yuma by following the Colorado River.

There were many soldiers on the steamer. We were told not to look out on the great water because we were sure to get sick. We got up on the steamer and I was near the top, which had a glass roof. The other two boys were below. We were on board for a few days, and one of the boys was sick, throwing up yellow and green foam and hardly able to stand up. Some of the soldiers took care of him and gave him some whiskey, and he got over it in a couple of days. The reason he got sick was that he always wanted to watch the giant waves and the white foam the water makes.

At last we were at the Gulf of California and changed to a smaller steamer. This time we didn't see any waves or white foam, just red water. That must have been the Colorado River, on whose banks the Yumas and Mojaves lived.

Four hard days of pulling brought us to Yuma, and on the east side the boat stopped and put off Mr. Coke and the three Pimas, who traveled home along the Gila River. We had to go on to La Paz, where Dr. McNeil got an outfit ready and brought us to Wickenburg. In a few more days we finally reached home and saw our people again. We had been gone about seven months. We left in November 1870, and when we returned it was the beginning of summer.

8

Nahtahdavbah and other chiefs of the Mojave Indians hatched a conspiracy to have the soldiers arrest the Yavapais who were camping at Camp Date Creek. They arranged it this way: Nahtahdavbah and Ahsojithaw would give a plug of tobacco to each of the Indians whom they wanted to see arrested, and with that signal the soldiers could take their prisoners.

Eight Yavapai chiefs were taken captive this way, marched off with a soldier on each side. The rest of the Indians couldn't understand why they were treated this way, but they didn't make a fuss about it.

Three broke loose from the soldiers and managed to get away beyond shooting distance, and even though two were wounded, they were all right afterward. The other four were killed right there. Just at that moment José Pakota arrived from Washington, where he had met with President Grant and agreed that there would be no more hostilities among any people, no matter whether they be white, black, red, or yellow. When he heard about this great tragedy, he went to the commanding officer of the post, who was Captain James Burns, and showed him the papers and the medal with the face of President Grant, and after Burns had read the papers and looked at the picture, he apologized that such things had been done to his people, but he wanted him to understand that his command had not done the deed. Rather, it was soldiers who had come from Fort Mojave, where they had been influenced by the three Mojave leaders. Captain Burns said he did not believe that the Indians had done anything wrong, because he had followed their trail to this camp, and they had stayed in camp and had obeyed when they were told not to leave without a written pass that stated for what purpose they were going away from Camp Date Creek. No one had come to him for permission yet, he said, and he had ordered that the Indians be counted every week, which had been done for several months without any absentees being reported.

Gen. George R. Crook (1829–90). An
expert Indian fighter, Crook spent the
last years of his life speaking out against
injustices done to Native American
peoples.

Even so, Nahtahdavbah insisted that he was certain that no one
else had done the awful killings, and so he had wanted these chiefs to
be killed in turn in his presence. Somehow General George Crook,
who was the commander of the military department, agreed with the
three blackguard Mojaves' story, and he allowed those innocent men
to be punished with death right in front of their people.

Nahtahdavbah did all these things to protect himself and the Mojave people against the wrongs he had done to the whites. The Yumas
and the Mojaves were the first Indians the whites had trouble with in
Arizona, and those troubles kept on. The Maricopas, who lived near
Gila Crossing just above where the Oatman family and others were
slaughtered, had often told stories about killings committed by Mojaves from the Colorado River. Some Maricopas were traveling along
the Gila River and happened upon the bodies of some white people.
They followed the trail, and noticed many clubs and arrows that were
of a different style from the Apache ones. The Maricopas knew that
the Apaches didn't use clubs, which are made of cut ironwood, and
they noticed that the footprints were square at the toes and were very
large, bigger than Apache ones. They wanted to be sure, so they followed the trail for some distance across the desert, heading along
until they reached the foothills above the Colorado River, and so they
were satisfied that the Mojaves had committed the slaughter.

I'm not sure that this great tragedy was ever solved. The only thing
that was said was that Nahtahdavbah massacred the whites and then
pretended to be friends with them, hiding all the bloody things he
had done and blaming them on the poor innocent Apaches, who in

those days would never have seen a white man. For that reason we were massacred, first near the Superstition Mountains, then at Skull Valley, and then on many occasions, and if I knew the exact number of the dead I would write it down. We were thought of as bloodthirsty, but the Apaches have human feelings toward other people. The Apaches were pushed and forced to protect themselves and their families. I think very little of a man who does not try to protect his own rights. This is just what the Apaches did, with bows and arrows that they made themselves.

After the four chiefs were killed at Camp Date Creek, the rest of the Indians were escorted to Camp Verde. Only a few months later, General Crook wanted them all to enlist in the army as scouts. There were about eighty-five Apache Yumas and Apache Mojaves enlisted. There came a company of cavalry under Lieutenant E. D. Thomas, and Lieutenant H. S. Bishop led G Troop of the Fifth Cavalry from Fort Whipple. They were ordered to go up toward the north to follow Hualapai chief Surauma, who had reportedly been leading parties that made some raids a little west of Skull Valley. The trails went north, in any case. So José Pakota, who had just come back from Washington, was chosen chief under Thomas and Bishop. They went to the Hualapai country, and the first camp they reached was Walapai Charlie's. He said he had nothing to do with it, but that his brother Surauma was the one who did everything they claimed he did, and that they should follow Surauma wherever he might go until they caught him.

The scouting parties under Thomas and Bishop followed the hostiles toward the Colorado River. There must have been a lot of them, because they made a trail as large as a wagon road. At last the command came to a camp, and the ashes were still hot. They continued to the rim of the Colorado River, where a fight took place. They killed three Indians, and even though they didn't capture Surauma they did take many families prisoner and turned them over to the command at Fort Mojave.

Many bloody deeds were done by people who were not Apaches. All the same, the Apaches were taken to Camp Verde and Cottonwood. When the Hualapais came to Skull Valley and drove away some cattle, they probably wanted to make it seem as if the Apaches had done it, but the Apaches were far away, and this time the soldiers were watching. So it was that General Crook knew that the Apaches were not to blame, and he called them up to be scouts. Another hundred or so came from the Tonto people from the east.

At about that time, some of the Apaches who were at San Carlos broke out and headed up over the Superstitions and the Salt River to the Four Peaks. The Tonto scouts were under a German named Al Sieber, who had become acquainted with General Crook. The Tontos went down the Verde River to Fort McDowell. There some soldiers joined them, with Lieutenant Walter S. Schuyler of the Fifth Cavalry in charge and William H. Corbusier, the surgeon. They started off toward the Four Peaks and made a camp in the foothills. The scouts reported some hostile tracks leading to the north side of the Peaks.

The scouts under Sieber were ordered to follow the tracks. Nearly all of the scouts went, though none of the soldiers did. They found an Indian camp before sunup and fired on it from some distance away, but without any effect. Many of the enemy shot back, and it was clear that they were well armed; they stood their ground, while the women and children moved only a short distance away. The scouts shot until they ran out of ammunition in late afternoon, and then they were ordered to retreat and get more. They went back to camp and had something to eat, then returned to the battleground. They were careful, because the hostiles knew they were out and about.

There were ten or twelve Indians there who had enlisted with the scouts at San Carlos and got away from that place with the stragglers following the great chief Delshe, whose roaming country was the Four Peaks and Superstitions. Some of these runaway scouts had old Henry rifles that had seven cartridges plus one in the muzzle, making eight, and could fire just as fast as a Winchester nowadays.

At about dawn the next morning the Apache Yuma scouts came on the camp again. They opened fire and kept on firing. Al Sieber was at the head, but still there were no soldiers. The hostiles had taken a strong position on bluffs just above the camp, and when the scouts entered the camp to search it, the hostiles poured in a volley at them. You would laugh to see all those well-armed fellows in a clump trying to get away from the camp, so frightened that they nearly dropped their guns. Only a few were hurt.

After a while they renewed the fight. It lasted two days, and when it ended they could not find any of the women or children. They found three of the runaway scouts dead in the camp, along with lots of bloodstains and a tooth that had fallen from someone's jaw.

One of the Apache scouts strayed away, scared to join his comrades. He intended to go home, or else to Camp Verde. He came across two Indian women traveling by themselves, and he hid behind a bush and demanded their surrender, thinking that he could take them as prisoners back to camp and show that he had done something in the battle. He was an Apache Mojave, and his name was Poulgayaiya, which means "whitish forehead," so that he might have had some grayish hair when he was a child, for an Indian child is always named for something noticeable or worthy of a name. He was distantly related to the two women, it's said, and they believed him when he said he wouldn't hurt them, that he only wanted to take them to Camp Verde as protection. He kept a close eye out on the two captured women, whose names were Sicooyah (shiny place) and Ceeyatay (many girls), all night long and didn't sleep a wink.

The next day they went on, and at noon they reached the Verde River. They agreed to take a rest. The man sat down under a cottonwood tree and in a few minutes fell asleep, dropping his gun. The two young women said to themselves that it was time for them to make an escape, and one of them said, "Let's mash this man's head in with a big stone and then take his gun and give it to our people." Instead, though, they agreed that if they missed he would kill them, so they just stole away from the man, looking back from time to time to see if he was still asleep and then running as fast as they could. They ran off toward a bluff, and when they got away to the top they heard some gunshots coming from the direction of the man they had left. The two Apache Mojave women found some of their relatives on the east side of the Four Peaks, the sharp-looking mountains. That was all they knew about the man who took them and whom they promised to accompany to Camp Verde.

The rest of the Yuma scouts went to Fort McDowell with some captives, and then a few days later they went to Camp Verde, where they turned the captives over to the soldiers. The scouts who had gone toward the Pinal Mountains and the San Carlos Agency had not met any enemies, and it was reported at Fort McDowell that the Apaches who had left San Carlos had returned to the reservation. They had been following a Pinal Apache chief who traveled with some younger chiefs. These men dared him to kill a white man someday, since the old man was always talking about how he had killed enemies in the past. He told them not to talk that way, since in the old days everyone was hungry but now there was plenty of beef, flour, sugar, and coffee for anyone who settled down at peace along the Gila bottomlands or at the San Carlos Agency. This kind of talk did no good, and the old man got angry because the young people did not agree with him.

They met other people at a place where there was a lot of drinking going on. The drink was made out of sprouted corn. It foams just like beer, and when it gets just right it tastes stronger than beer. It gets people very drunk, and the chiefs were getting funny drinking this stuff.

Some of the people there took to laughing at the old chief, saying that they had killed plenty of soldiers. They dared him again to go kill a white man, since there were lots of them around. He asked them if they meant what they said, and they answered yes. So the old chief and some other chiefs went down to where some freighters who were hauling goods to San Carlos had made camp. The wagons were loaded with all kinds of stuff, including several cases of whiskey. The chief went off toward the freighters, and soon shots rang out. The others went there and found four white men lying dead and all the wagons afire except the one that carried the whiskey. Some of the Indians started drinking straight out of the barrel, while others filled their ollas and carried them off to the hills as fast as they could. Some were still drinking around the burning wagons. They got so drunk that they couldn't even remember the old chief's name.

The Indians were lucky because the Gila was very high and rising. Even though there were four companies of cavalry stationed at San Carlos, the soldiers couldn't cross the river to save the freighters. Otherwise the Indians would have been slaughtered, since they were so drunk they couldn't even walk. Instead, they lay on the side of the road under the bushes.

Finally they sobered up. They went across to Hog Canyon and made up their minds to continue what they were doing, going down to the San Pedro Valley and killing whomever they found and stealing whatever they could. So they went down to the San Pedro and killed two men, one white and one Mexican, and got many cattle and some horses. Looking over at the Gila from the mountains, they saw that the water was still high. This made some of them very brave. But others, who were completely over their drunk, knew that the water would get low someday, and so they went back toward San Carlos and sent word to the agent that they wanted to come home and draw rations, saying that they thought it was a bad policy to steal from poor people and kill them.

The agent replied that they must go back and find the chiefs, kill them, and bring their heads back to the reservation. Then they could come live there, but not until then.

At the fight between the Apache Mojaves and the Apache Yumas on the Four Peaks, one of the Yuma scouts got shot through the jaw while he was hollering to the others. The bullet went through his mouth and came out just below his ear, but it only broke off a tooth. His name was Nattoomoorgecha, which means "scratching." He was taken to the hospital at Fort McDowell and was finally well enough to return to Camp Verde. Most of the other scouts went to Camp Verde as well. That man Poulgayaiya, who had taken the two women prisoners when he strayed away from his comrades, went back to Camp Verde, but he never reported to the commanders or went to see about his pay. He was afraid that the soldiers would ask why he had been traveling alone, and he never let on that he was in the service.

These Indian scouts were tough. They knew the way over the rough hills just as we did, knew all the waterholes and campsites. We gave ourselves up to them, not to the soldiers. The Pinal and Tonto Apaches went off to San Carlos, while other people under Bowwatay (Big Gun) agreed to follow the trail of the scouts and go to Camp Verde. The two groups of Indians bid each other good-bye and cried to think of their country deserted by its inhabitants. Once they had lived at peace all over this land, unmolested and unafraid, going all kinds of distances to gather food without having to worry about enemies. They were ours, the valleys, gulches, hills, and mountainsides, the springs, the creeks, and the riverlands, where all kinds of green trees grew, filled with wildflowers and game herds and food and herbs.

9

In time, everyone came to be hunting for those four chiefs. Within a year three of them had been killed. Only one, a man named Ichtahatchja, was still alive, and he hid away. He was a hard man to catch. Once he went in to San Carlos and killed a white sergeant and then got away before he was caught.

But even he didn't last. His own nephew was responsible. This young man met his uncle, crying, and told him that he was the only one of his people who was still alive; all the others had been slaughtered, and he was just wandering through the countryside looking for someone to be a comfort to him. He had had nothing to eat for a week since his family and all his people had been killed—not by white soldiers, but by Yuma scouts.

None of this was true, but the old man began to cry. He knew that there was a camp of about seventy-five scouts only half a mile away, and after a while he asked his nephew to go there with him. After drying off his face, the old man started off over a hill, the young man a few yards behind him. Then the nephew took out a pistol that he had hidden under his shirt and shot the old chief right through the back of his head. When the old man fell, he shot him again in the forehead to be sure that he was dead. He also wanted everybody in the camp to know that he had got the man, the last chief of the Aravaipa Apaches.

The Apaches made one of the Mojaves carry the head in a sack, and off they went to the agency. There must have been five thousand Apaches that went in with them. Others went in to Camp Verde, trusting that the officer in command would spare their lives. There Delshe's daring little band of thirty-seven was marched in two by two, each man chained to the other. They were kept that way for a long time, and when they were released they found that the Indian scouts had taken most of their women as wives.

Another chief was named Wepotehe, whose name means "big

broad shoulders." He died. His son was among the thirty-seven prisoners, and when he got the news of his father's death he escaped from the guards somehow and ran over the hills to near where Jerome is now.

That was in 1873. In that year, most of the Indians gathered in the Verde Valley at General Crook's call. The old Yavapais who used to live in the Bradshaw Mountains and Jerome Mountains were among them. The first chief who came in was from Walkayauayauyah, meaning "mountain full of pine trees," or "pine top." He was called Coquannathacka, meaning "green leaves." When he came in, he gave up all his weapons; he had only a bow and some arrows. Not many of his followers came with him apart from a sister, his wife, an uncle, and his uncle's brother and all their children. He was told to go back and tell all his people to come at once to Camp Verde, for General Crook commanded that the scattered bands of the Yavapais do so, since he had a place for them to live close to where the soldiers are, and the soldiers would give them food and clothing and would be their protectors as long as they lived where they were put. People were supposed to farm the land, not live in the wild like animals, hiding in the mountains. Only bad people live that way, and the Great Father in Washington wanted his Indian children not to steal or kill other people anymore, else he would have the soldiers out on every hill in the country hunting those who had not come in to give themselves up once they had been told to do so.

For there is no use trying to fight the Great Uncle Sam. White people are able to furnish their soldiers with everything they need to fight the Indians. The white people make all the guns and ammunition, while the Indians have sticks, or lances, or spears to fight with. So Coquannathacka and his band left their home, and other bands came in from the headwaters of Oak Creek, in what is called red rock country. These people are called Ewebookha, people of the caves, because the country is nothing but rocks and caves. It is supposed that the first Indian was born near these caves soon after the flood, and it is also said that you can see a child's footprint in some of the caves and some smooth level places where the child used to play.

After three or four bands gathered, runners were sent out toward the San Francisco Mountains, or what the Indians call Weemoonkawaw, meaning "a mountain that is always cold." Some came in from Bill Williams Mountain, or Jockawee, which means "that country is full of cedar trees." The Bill Williams band was headed by Teecoomthaya, a chief of all the Yavapais.

They all came down to Camp Verde. General Crook had selected as chief a man called Mojave Charlie who came from the red rock country. Many of the Yavapais disputed the choice, saying that he wasn't the right man for the job, because he wasn't inclined to make peace with the soldiers. But still old chief Coquannathacka said that he did not care to become the head of the people. For one thing, he wasn't much of a talker, not as much as the man Crook selected. Mojave Charlie was given a major's uniform and a saber to wear. He had a black hat and yellow stripes on his pants.

There was another chief selected to be captain over the Apache Yumas who came over from Date Creek. This man's name was Chemawalasela. He commanded all the Indians belonging to the Yuma tribe, from the western country. Lieutenant E. D. Thomas of G Troop, Fifth US Cavalry, escorted them from Date Creek to Camp Verde in the summer of 1873.

Some bands did not keep up with the rest of the 3,500 men, women, and children of the Tolkepayas, or Apache Yumas, as they were called. About thirty-five families left their relatives and went off down into the desert, off toward the Colorado River, and they have never been on a reservation even today. They don't bother anyone. Several years afterward they went to some settlements and mining camps and worked there. In this way they lived well without any aid from the government. Most of them can speak English, and the younger men can also read and write. They handle their own affairs and deal with all kinds of people down at Congress Junction, and Congress and Wickenburg, and Skull Valley and Kirkland. Some of the young men were employed as miners, cowboys, and farmhands, and they dressed and ate as well as anyone. That goes to show that if Indians were not molested or imposed on, they would all live like that, and work to bring themselves food and clothing and pick up other languages, English and Spanish.

Some of the Yavapais gathered at Bill Williams Mountain. There were about seventy-five families in the camp with head chief

Teecoomthaya, and they were unconcerned about soldiers bothering them. So a party of twenty-five young men went to Supai country. Some had made friends there earlier by giving the people presents. One young man was called Pelhaymu, or Old Man's Foot. He had given a Havasupai a mule a few years earlier, while others had given many buckskins in friendship. So the Havasupais—the name means "people of the green water"—were friendlier toward the Yavapais than the Hualapais were. The young men with Pelhaymu agreed to go down to the Havasupai settlement, taking along some buckskins as presents. They reached the settlement at night, and a friendly old Havasupai told them that he was sorry to hear the news that the Hualapais had enlisted in the army to go over into Yavapai country to kill anyone they saw, and that white soldiers were coming up from the south to do the same.

The Havasupais gave their Yavapai visitors some guns and lots of gunpowder so that they could protect themselves. No sooner had they heard the sad news than did they return the way they came, not even making camp on the way home, but instead traveling over rough country all night long. The next day at noon someone saw smoke rising over Bill Williams Mountain, in the same direction as where they had left the main body of the Yavapais. Chief Teecoomthaya told them to hurry over the mountains and be on the lookout for enemies, for he had been told that there were all kinds of soldiers in their country. The young fast runners had already reached a spot near the old camp and saw that the country and the campsite had been burned up. They met some Indians who told them that the Huala-pais had come right into the village and shot down almost everyone before they knew what was happening. A few people in the camp had seen the Hualapais coming and said that they were enemies, but others said that they were just the Yavapais who had gone to visit their friends over in Supai country. They argued back and forth about this until the Hualapai soldiers arrived and began shooting. Even the men in the camp made no attempt to protect themselves or the people.

The Hualapais inflicted a great blow on the Yavapais that day. They attacked without the least warning, not even giving them the choice of making peace or fighting to the last man. Orders had been given to the white soldiers and Indian scouts that if they came across any body of Indians they first had to demand their surrender; if they didn't surrender, then they would all be killed, so the best policy was to surrender.

When the runners arrived, the Hualapais must have left only a few hours before. There were dead bodies everywhere, so badly burned that they could not be recognized. No one could count how many had been killed. Some of those who escaped said that they had seen others going over the hills with children, so some families may have been saved.

Some of the men wanted to chase the invaders, but the chief told them not to be so foolish as to start a fight with a much stronger enemy; the Hualapais were better armed, and they had white soldiers to back them up. They decided instead to go into the country, where they hoped their missing families were likely to be found. They scattered into the countryside until they heard noises, crying, off in the direction of a deep gulch. This was near nightfall. And they found some of their lost families. Some of the women had gotten all their children out safely, but other women had lost many. A few men were also missing from their families.

Together they mourned their lost relatives.

This was the first surprise attack on the Yavapais. No one expected any danger, because they hadn't done anything to strangers and expected the same treatment in return; otherwise they would have been on the lookout for enemies and would have been prepared for an attack. The whole band was left desolate. Not only were their relatives murdered, but they also might just as well have been left naked, and they had to go to the San Francisco Mountains and over to the Hopi settlements to be given clothing and other things to start them off in life again. They went to the banks of the Little Colorado River, where they happened to meet some of their people living with many Tonto Apache families. Instead of going on to Hopi country, they decided to stay with the Apaches, who gave them blankets, food, and whatever else they needed. This was over toward the Mogaume Mountains and the headwaters of the East River.

One evening three young men came into the camp and told the Indians to gather, because they had big news. A chief's camp was selected for the meeting. The three young men told the people that there was a great chief who had come to Camp Verde. He had a long white beard but looked like an old woman, because his face was so wrinkled and his eyes were so small. This chief wore a brown canvas coat. He had come there with many soldiers, both Indian and white, and officers to make a campaign against Indians who stayed out in the countryside once they had been called onto the reservation by this great general. He was General George Crook, the commander of all the soldiers in Arizona.

10

General Crook sent runners out to all the people to tell them to stay close to Camp Verde, saying that they would be given all the food they wanted, along with blankets, calicos, corn, and wheat and barley seeds to plant on the bottomlands.

All the headmen of the different bands got together and talked about what was best to do, and they decided to come within a week's time. In the meantime, some of their young men went out hunting deer and antelope and happened to notice great lines of horsemen at some distance. They came to notify the others. Most all of the Indians broke camp and went toward the Verde River, the opposite direction from where the soldiers were heading.

The three young men returned to Camp Verde to tell General Crook that in four or five days there would be a great number of Indians coming in. They told him that when the Indians left their camps there would be lots of smoke from their fires, and they asked that the soldiers meet them outside the post.

Some people from the red rocks were the first to arrive. Barsukae-laelah had been their head chief. He had come to the post some time before and was put in the guardhouse for attempting to stab the commanding officer. The way it happened was this. Those three young men had been rounded up earlier and sent off to Prescott, where General Crook was stationed. The interpreter, a man named Joe Gacka, whose father was a Mojave and mother a Yavapai, told him that the three young men had gone home to the mountains. Barsukaelaelah knew that this was a lie, and he said that the whites had better tell him the truth or he would make them pay. The commanding officer told him the same story, saying that the three young men had gone home, told to gather up the people and bring them here to live near the post and be fed by his men. The more Barsukaelaelah was told that the three men had returned to their homes, the angrier he grew. He got so mad that he jumped up, grabbed the officer by the throat, and made a motion to pull his knife out. Two or three officers standing nearby disarmed him and dragged him to the guardhouse. When the rest of the Indians heard what had happened, they went off to the mountains in the middle of the night and were past the red rock country by morning.

About two weeks later, Barsukaelaelah caught a guard and tried to take his gun from him. Another soldier shot him and killed him. If he had been told the truth, that the three young men had been taken prisoner and sent to Prescott, then he would have gone there to try to negotiate with General Crook to have them released.

But that was the way government commanders dealt with Indians. I know of many similar cases but would not like to say too much about it.

The people did not know what had happened to Barsukaelaelah, and about three thousand Yavapais and Tontos came in from the Tonto Basin. Several hundred more had already come in from the ranges near Squaw Peak in the south and the Bloody Basin and east of the Agua Fria. The soldiers took all the men and paraded them before the commanding general, then marched them to the guardhouse just so they could claim that they had captured all the renegade bands of Apaches. There must have been about ten thousand men, women, and children besides the Apache Yumas, who had come in from the west. They were all told to go out four or five miles into the hills and cut cedar and bring the wood to the post. They brought back several thousand cords of wood on their backs and were met by soldiers who gave some of them banknotes, others blankets, and still others corn.

At about that time another fifteen hundred men, women, and children from the south came in. Their chief was Motha, or Cloud. A man had been sent out to them. He must have been an agent, because he didn't dress like an army officer. He had a black suit and a large black hat, and so the Indians called the white man "Big Black Hat."

It happened that a few families did not come in, for no one had gotten the word to them. The women had been gathering walnuts on the bottomlands of Ash Creek, near where the power lines cross it today, while the men hunted antelope and small game and the children played in the meadows. At noon they saw some smoke toward their main camp, and when they climbed a high hill they saw that the camp was on fire. Some of the young men wanted to go there, but they were persuaded that it would mean certain death, since there were more than a hundred soldiers in the valley. They could see that the soldiers had some children on their saddles. They were marching back toward the Agua Fria and Prescott. One girl had been shot in the arm, and a boy had been shot in the leg.

The soldiers made camp at the Agua Fria and, spying some Indians in the hills, saw that they had been followed. Twelve soldiers crept through the willows on the river bottom and over a hill, and they saw six Indian men lying on the ground looking down toward the soldiers' camp. The soldiers were about three hundred yards away. They opened fire and killed four Indians with their first shots. The other two ran but were shot to pieces.

One of the Indians was a chief. He wore a dressy buckskin shirt and pants. The soldiers took the clothes with them, and the children recognized them immediately, for two of the chief's children were among the captives. The chief's aged mother had also been killed, and the chief was crazed with anger. He hoped to kill soldiers, but he met his death instead, and so did the young men who followed him.

The soldiers broke camp, having killed plenty of Indians and taken six children captive. They took the children to Fort Whipple, and the doctors attended to the wounded ones. They cut the girl's arm off and fixed her. One night she got away and went back to her people not far from where she had been captured.

Two of the children died. Two boys were raised by some good lady and afterward moved to the agency at San Carlos in 1874. One of them was named Mojave Dick, and he was employed as an interpreter for the Mojaves and Apache Yumas. The other boy became a scout for the agency. Mojave Dick died in a peculiar manner: he sometimes sat outside his tepee naked, and even when he was told to put on his clothes he didn't pay any attention, and for several days he would go without eating. In this manner he died of starvation. The other boy, whose name I don't remember, died of an unknown disease. His grandmother cared for him and received his pay for some time after his death.

The last of the children was raised by a rancher named Bowers, who had a place near Dewey that was only a ruin, and another place near Prescott. He named the boy Jim Bowers. He stayed with Bowers's family for several years after all the Yavapais, Yumas, and Tontos were taken over to the San Carlos Agency. The boy went there to look for his parents but was told that they had died of fever at Cottonwood on the Verde River. He found his grandmother still alive, married to another man. His name was Wilgaikilcovah, meaning "tying his throat," and he was the man who killed Leihy, the agent of the Colorado Mojaves, near Kirkland, close to the place where so many Indians were killed.

So most all of the Indians had gathered at Camp Verde by this time. They cut wood, and the women were paid with cups of corn. The Apache Yumas selected some of their young men to enlist in the army to go out with the soldiers to fight the Apaches who were still in the hills. Lieutenant Charles King was out with a detachment, A Troop of the Fifth US Cavalry, stationed at Camp Verde. He had twelve Apache Yuma scouts. The little command marched out toward Stoneman Lake, and two or three of the Yumas were ordered to scout through the country to see if they could find any tracks of the renegade Apaches. They returned without any good news, but they did come across where some mescal had been burned what looked to be several weeks before.

The next day the command moved camp toward the Little Colorado River, following an old wagon road, and Lieutenant King told the scouts to be on watch for Apaches. The company came to a little running spring and saw fresh moccasin prints. Lieutenant King halted and ordered the soldiers and scouts to eat without building a fire and to prepare themselves for action. Then, instead of taking all of them, he went with one sergeant and five scouts to ascend a mountain. When they got near the top the trail was fresher, and there must have been a whole tribe standing there on top of a mesa watching their movements the whole time. The Yumas crouched down, expecting shooting any minute, but the lieutenant and sergeant kept on going as if nothing was happening; the sergeant had his gun strapped to his saddle, and the lieutenant's pistol was fastened in its holster. Shots rang out, and the lieutenant dropped from his horse, which ran away. The Indian scouts were firing at the bluffs, but they could not see any Apaches. Presently the sergeant came running out from the foot of the bluffs without a pistol or rifle. If he was any fighter at all he would have been prepared for an emergency, since, after all, they were following fresh tracks. But I suppose he was a young man with no experience in war, especially against Apaches, who will take whatever advantage they can whenever they can.

The Indian scouts saw the lieutenant running down the rough rocky hill as fast as his feet could touch the ground, but he was weak, and when he got to some cedar brush he fell to the ground. One of the five scouts volunteered to go over to him and hide him, and he told the rest of the scouts to fire as fast as they could to give him cover. Bawnagoo was the scout who saved Lieutenant Charles King, even though the sergeant received a medal for gallantry for doing the saving. What happened was this: Bawnagoo went over to the officer, who was lying face down, and got hold of his arm. The arm was broken, and King hollered out. Bawnagoo rolled him over and saw that his eyes were moving rapidly, as if he were dying. The officer motioned for him to stay close by and for him to take his ammunition belt. King took all the cartridges out of his belt and threw them down on the ground and told the scout to shoot with them, but the scouts all carried .44 caliber Henry rifles and the soldiers had .50 caliber guns, so the cartridges were useless, since the lieutenant had dropped his gun.

The sergeant found King's gun when he came running down from the bluffs. His own gun was still tied to his saddle. His horse was grazing close by the scouts. The sergeant ordered the scouts to fire at any Indians they saw and then went dashing down the hill at a dead run. The camp was only a mile away, and the other soldiers couldn't have helped hearing the shots; in fact, the scouts could hear the soldiers issuing commands, mounting up, and riding up the hill in twos and fours and single file. When they came to where the Indian scouts were waiting, they pulled their guns from their saddles and pointed them right at them. The soldiers dismounted and came up to the Indian scouts and pushed them away as though they wanted to shoot those poor friendly Indians. But instead of the twenty-five fresh-bodied soldiers going up over the hill, they pushed the Indian scouts on and pointed to the hills; they wanted to follow the scouts. The scouts left Lieutenant King with five soldiers and climbed over the mesa, the soldiers following them, and when they got to the top they didn't see any Indians, only some prickly pears and mescal fruits under the cedar trees where they must have made a temporary camp.

The scouts saw that there had been about thirty-five or fifty families among them, and perhaps seventy-five warriors. Only about seven of them actually fired at the scouts and soldiers, while the others were out on a hunting party. They were good shots, and the Apache Yumas saved Lieutenant King's life. But he made no effort to give any credit to the scouts for saving him. Four soldiers carried him back to camp, and then three soldiers went back to Camp Verde to get a doctor. It took about three days, and then a doctor named Davis, who was with General Crook, came out in a buggy and got him.

The scouts came back and reported that the trail was leading to the Little Colorado River, though some of the Indians had scattered when they saw that soldiers were coming. These were Tonto Apaches who lived on the Mogollon Rim, north of where Payson is now. A detachment of soldiers and scouts was sent off to head them off. The men traveled day and night, and on the second night out Cubbohaiya, the Indian sergeant of scouts, was badly hurt. He was so honored by the soldiers and officers that he was given a mule to ride, while all the other Apache Yuma scouts had to travel on foot, and the mule got scared and threw him on his face. Cubbohaiya landed on the point of a stone that stuck between his eyes, and he was so stunned that everyone thought he was dead. He came around, but the blood flowed so thickly that he could hardly see to travel. The soldiers left him by the side of the road with some bread, coffee, sugar, and water and traveled on. The scouts who had been following on foot caught up with him and found him with a hole in his forehead that you could put a finger through, his eyes so swollen that he couldn't see. The soldiers hadn't cared whether he lived or died or got caught by hostile Indians. He was an Indian, too, but the hostiles would have killed him just as they would have killed any soldier they came across. It was his good luck that his own people found him and led him on to the soldiers' next camp.

The next morning one of the scouts was ordered to take Cubbohaiya back to Camp Verde, while the others were told to hunt for signs of Indian tracks. Almost all of them could see that there were tracks at a little spring of water, real fresh tracks made by Indians who kneeled there for a drink. The scouts tried to make the soldiers understand that hostiles were close, but the soldiers acted as if they didn't care. This is just the way that the sergeant and Lieutenant King

A group of Apache scouts in
about 1880. The US Army
employed Indian scouts
in nearly every campaign
during the Indian Wars.

had followed the trail up the hill and Lieutenant King had got his
arm shot off.

I knew that Dr. Davis back at Fort Whipple in 1873. He often came
to Captain Burns's house when he got sick, and afterward there was a
Dr. Matthew, who was the post doctor. Neither doctor was of much
help to him. Captain Burns died after crossing the Little Colorado
River near Navajo Springs and was buried at Fort Wingate, New
Mexico. He was on his way home to Washington on sick leave. The
doctors had done him no good, and they thought a change of climate
might help him. So he was going home with his wife, Annie Burns.
They had two children, a boy and a girl. Later, some soldiers escorted
Mrs. Burns to a post in Kansas. I learned long afterward that Mrs.
Burns died and her two children had grown up, but I was never able
to see them to let them know that I was one of the Burns family.
Captain Burns had adopted me into his family the same as one of his
own children and was going to take me along with him to his mother
and father's home in Ireland. I do believe that I never would have
seen the land of my own mother and father again. Lieutenant H. S.
Bishop, the second lieutenant of G Troop, Fifth US Cavalry, showed
me where Captain Burns was buried, and I wept bitterly because I
respected him as much as my father. I was raised by him while I was
only a child.

When Dr. Davis arrived to treat Lieutenant King, the whole command left for Camp Verde. Lieutenant King was put into the buggy,
and a two-day march brought them home. The Indian scouts were
told to keep their guns and remain near Cottonwood as guards.
There were Yumas, Yavapais, Mojaves, and Tontos. The first three

tribes can speak the same tongue, but the Tontos speak a different language entirely.

When the Yavapais first came in to Camp Verde, they camped just across from the post. Then four headmen were arrested and put in chains for stealing cattle and horses, something that had been done around Chino Valley, Kirkland Valley, and Wickenburg. There was no verification of the accusation. They were innocent people who were tired of living the rough life out in the woods and wanted to live on the bottomland. For that reason they had come to Camp Verde of their own accord to make treaty terms with the soldiers. When their leaders were taken, the Yavapais did not ask for the reason. The whole camp just made haste for the mountains from which they came. Then came some Tontos under a chief named Charlie Chapan. There must have been seven thousand of them. Then some Mojaves came from the southwest. Some came from the Bradshaw Mountains. More Mojaves came from the mountains where Jerome is now, and others came from the red rock country and the headwaters of Oak Creek. Then Delshe's band came in, and all forty-seven of the men were put in chains and had been like that for about six months. Yumas came in from Date Creek, and other Indians came from the country around Bill Williams Mountain and Flagstaff, and Tontos came in from the eastern country. The headmen of all those bands got together and had a talk with the officers, and soon the forty-seven men and the four headmen were released from the guardhouse at the order of General George Crook, who was commander of the Department of the West.

II

This is the way the soldiers rounded up the Apaches. There has been much said about the soldiers conquering them by fighting them, but the only place where they had a fight was at the Battle of the Caves on Salt River—we call it the Bloody Salt River Cave Massacre—in December 1872. The Indians came in willingly. General Crook had come to Camp Verde to have a conference with all of the Apaches gathered there, and he gave to the headman of each band a written paper telling them to keep it as long as they lived, that the spoken words would be forgotten but the written words would last forever. One of these papers was given to Mojave Charlie, and when he died his nephew, Marshall Pete, who succeeded him as chief, received it. Part of it is as follows:

> I want to have all you say here go down on paper, be written with pen and ink, because what goes down on paper never dies. A man's memory may fail him, but what the paper tells will be fresh and true long after we are all dead and forgotten. This will not bring back the dead but what is put down on this paper today may help the living. What I want to get at is all that has happened since I left here to bring about this trouble, this present condition of affairs. I want you to tell the truth without fear, and to tell it in as few words as possible, so that everybody can read it without trouble.

Marshall Pete was killed by Tonto Lewis, who had a grudge against the Apache Mojaves, and he crept up and shot Pete in the back of the head. Tonto Lewis was half Tonto and half Mojave. He had married into the Chiricahuas and was sent to Florida with them—about eight hundred of them were rounded up—and it was two years before he was released and sent back to Arizona. He had it in for the Apache

Mojaves, since they and the Apache Yumas had killed about thirty of the Tontos in a fight on the East Verde River, including some of his relatives.

General Crook told the Indians that he had been sent by General Grant—he was the president, the man who had freed the Negro people after having a war between the South and the Northern people—to make peace with the Indians, and that if any of them did not pay heed to his call he had a lot of soldiers who would get them from all over the country. All Indians who wanted peace, he said, had better come in and become friendly with the whites, in exchange for which they would have plenty of food and clothing as long as they remained at peace. They were to live in the right way on the bottomlands and raise grain, corn, barley, wheat, and other things in the way civilized people did, rather than live in the mountains and come down from time to time to steal things. The soldiers would protect them.

The soldiers, however, did as they chose. Innocent people came in to live near Camp Verde for protection, but their chiefs were taken from them at first sight. When all the Indians came to Camp Cottonwood, General Crook appointed all the chiefs and captains.

Long ago, the Yavapais were the Mountain Mojaves, and the bands of this once-mighty people were separated. The Hualapais moved north, but some went farther west and settled along the Colorado River. The Yumas did the same, and some of the Yavapais went down and settled along the Gila River to become the Maricopas. By the time they came together on the Verde River under the soldiers' command, these Indians were all quite different.

There were five Apache Mojave bands and two Apache Yuma bands at the Rio Verde Agency. The chief of the first Mojave band was Makwa, whose name means quail's top-knot; the second was Wehabesuwa, whose name means green stone; the third was Motha, Fog, also called Mojave Charlie; the fourth was Pakula, long or tall man; and the fifth was Coquannathacka, green leaf. The Apache Yuma chiefs were Captain José Pakota and Captain Snook. Captain José had had a great career and was one of the party who went to Washington in 1870 to hold a council with President Grant. He was also called Captain Coffee, because he drank a large pot of it at each meal. Coquannathacka was the most noted chief of all, head of the Tonto Apaches. The Tontos outnumbered all of the other bands, but some were married to Apache Mojave women, and some of the Apache Mojave men had married Tonto women. They were all different people, and they spoke different languages, with the same trouble that a white man meeting a Mexican has.

About a hundred and fifty Apache Mojaves and twenty-five Apache Yumas were enlisted as scouts to go against the Hualapais. Another hundred and fifty Tontos were enlisted to go back to their own country, as news had come from Fort Apache that some several hundred Apaches had been seen near Cibecue, said to be scattered bands of Tontos who did not go to the Verde. The Tontos were ordered to bring their people in and to kill anyone who resisted. They found some of those renegade Tontos near Cave Creek, had a fight with them, killed several, and captured a few women whom they took to Camp Verde. Three of the Tonto scouts were killed. One of the scout sergeants and his son drowned getting the women back to Camp Verde; it was said later that the sergeant was afraid to go to a place where there were so many Mojaves.

The Apache Mojaves and Apache Yumas went out with Lieutenant E. D. Thomas and Lieutenant H. S. Bishop and Troop G of the Fifth Cavalry from Fort Whipple and captured Saurama, the head chief of the Hualapais, who had been stealing stock and horses, murdering people, and blaming the Apaches for it even after they were on the reservation. The trails went north, and the Hualapai chief Charlie told the soldiers that the Apaches were the guilty ones, but General Crook was sure that the Hualapais were the guilty parties and for that reason enlisted the Apaches as scouts. When the people heard the news that their worst enemy had been captured, many of them got together and began to dance. They kept it up from that afternoon until the next morning over the victory of their young warriors. The old women stripped them of their loot, since it was believed that it would prove harmful to the young men if they kept the spoils they had taken. It was also the custom of the women to sing a war song and dance around the captives in a circle, and they enjoyed just such a dance.

At the Rio Verde Agency rations were issued daily to every Indian. Even a newborn was counted as one, its parents receiving full rations for it. The rations consisted of flour, sugar, coffee, beans, bacon, and fresh beef. The Tontos were very treacherous and caused much trouble. When rations were being issued, they would throw stones at the others until the soldiers interfered. Then the Apache Mojaves and the Apache Yumas were placed on the west side of the river, where Cottonwood now stands. The trouble became so great that one Yavapai left and went to the hills near the red rocks, his old stomping ground. The officers went after him with Tonto scouts, and when they found him the soldiers took the women and children, but turned the man over to the Tontos. Afterward his skeleton was found hanging on a walnut tree. The Yavapais could never understand why the Tontos should persecute them, since they had never given them cause to do so, but had instead helped them when they needed it. They formerly had traveled over the same country and had gone to war together to fight other tribes. After they were taken to the reservation, though, there were no more depredations.

At one time fifteen hundred of the Indians at Cottonwood took ill. The Indians believed that Dr. Josephus Williams, the agency's head, had put something in the beef to make them sick. They noticed that the doctor was always handling the rations, especially the beef, before it was issued to each family. They found a little piece of paper in the middle of a piece of meat, and they said that the doctor had sprinkled poison on it.

Then a medicine man died, and another medicine man saw in his visions that a young woman in one of the camps was possessed by many evil spirits and had caused that man to die. A brother of the dead man went to the woman and killed her. This woman had a father but no mother, and a young single man lived with them. The father did nothing about the killing, but the young man went to shoot the man who had killed the woman. He missed his aim and killed someone else by mistake. He then headed for the hills and left the old man, who was killed by someone else.

In another camp a boy died and the father blamed the mother, so he killed her. Shortly afterward disease spread all through the camps, and family after family died. General Crook's favorite chief, called Chemawalasela, died, and the whole camp turned out and killed eight women and four men. That caused a great deal of commotion, and the soldiers had to come and stop the slaughtering of the innocents. They arrested some of the chiefs and the interpreter for not informing them about how bad things were getting, and they took them to Camp Verde and put them in the guardhouse.

Many of the Indians went to the hills, where the medicine men could sing over them without being ordered to stop singing, hoping to get better, and afterward some were found dead in the foothills and gulches. Many believed that Dr. Williams had poisoned them because he was under orders to do so, to kill them off. But later they believed differently and said it must have been caused by the poor quality of food, since there were all sorts of worms in the flour and some of it was yellow instead of white, so they had to separate it from the fine flour. It must have cost the government a lot of money to feed all of those Indians, and the contractors and agents and freighters must have made a lot of money on the side by defrauding the Indians and the government.

The Yavapais were well settled and had raised a good crop of wheat, barley, and corn. They were planning to plant again when orders came for them to move to the San Carlos Indian Agency. General Crook had promised the Apache Yumas that when the Yavapais were tamed they could return to Date Creek, their old home, which would belong to them as long as they lived. This was only a verbal agreement, and the Indians had done as they said they would and carried out their part of it, even acting as scouts and guides for the soldiers and fighting their own people. Now General Crook wanted them all to move over to San Carlos to set an example to the wilder class of Indians over there, saying that they could return to their homes within seven years, possibly even five. His fine promises, however, were never carried out. Perhaps if he had lived they would have been.

He was a great general and conquered the Indians in less than two years. He gave them good advice and instruction, and was just and kind. They thought a good deal of him and when they learned of his death they cried; there was no other general in the army who would do as much for them. The Indians called him Old Woman's Face, not meaning any disrespect. It wasn't a bad name. It was just that his face was all wrinkles and his eyes were so small that they would sometimes be lost in them. Indians are in the habit of giving names from something they see about a person, so Old Woman's Face it was.

The Indians had been living there for two years and had been peaceful. They followed orders, and they never made any attempts to go out into the fine country surrounding them, full of green forests, and clear springs of water, and lakes. Now they had to leave their

A Kwevkepaya camp near Date Creek. The image probably dates to the 1870s.

home, which was already small—all of northwestern Arizona used to be their home. They never dreamed that they would have to do so. All this can be traced back to the time when Columbus landed in America. He met many people, and they worshipped him and were glad to see him. They gave him everything he asked for. And then on his last visit he asked to take some of the chiefs home with him, promising that they would come back soon. But the chiefs never came home.

From that time on, and maybe before that, the Indians would destroy the belongings of people who had disappeared. That belief may have been handed down from the first woman, for the many tribes of Indians who call themselves Apache belong to the same family, being descended from one woman, Kowidema Pukeweh, or, old woman has power from the earth. This story was told to us by Coyote. It was at the time of a flood that a big tree was cut down, hollowed out nearly through, and she was told to get in, and into the hole she went, when it was stopped up. She had been warned not to look out until she heard the canoe strike against some rocks or trees. She did as she was told, and when she came out, she found that the canoe was lying on the top of the San Francisco Peaks, or somewhere near there. Nya, the sun, showed that lone woman, who was the only human being, what to eat and how to survive. He often visited her, and soon she bore him a daughter, who also had a son with Nya, Amjakupukah, which means "going around on the earth." Her mother told her that she must go far every day for training and exercise and to get things, for if she did not she would be useless, and she went so far one day that she was taken alive by a great *ah-sa*, or eagle, which carried her to its nest high up in a cliff of rocks in the mountains. There a young eagle ate her up, so the little boy had to be cared for by the grandmother until he learned to shoot bows and arrows. She taught him how to make them, what kind of wood to use, and how to tip the arrows with flint, put feathers on the shafts, and make bowstrings from the sinew of animals.

In those days, all the living creatures on the earth understood one another. The boy once came across an *ah-hoo-ma*, or quail, which he shot, breaking her leg. Ah-hoo-ma cried out and asked him not to hurt her anymore, but to fix her broken leg instead. If he did, she would tell him something that his own grandmother had never told him. He healed the bird with a touch, and then the quail asked him if his grandmother had ever told him what had happened to his mother. The boy said no. He asked the quail to tell him, because he had often wondered about that very thing. The quail told him of the sad affair of his mother and how she was eaten up by the eagles.

After he heard the story from the kind quail, he returned to the place where his grandma lived and she was preparing something for him to eat, but he was very sad and did not answer her calls. The next day he went off without eating anything, searching for the great eagle. Soon he heard what he thought was thunder, but it was the noise made by the eagle's wings overhead. He fell on his back, and the eagle caught him with her great claws and carried him in the same way as she did his mother. The boy looked so small that she immediately turned him over to her young ones to eat. Then she went away. The young eagles were turning his body over when he whistled to them and told them that he was their brother and said not to hurt him, but instead to tell him where the father eagle sat when he came home and what time of day both the old ones would be there, threatening to throw them over the bluff if they did not tell him. They told him, and when the two big ones came home he killed them.

At last he went back to his old grandmother's place, where he found her almost dead of grief at the loss of her only grandson, since she thought that he had been taken in the same way that his mother had been and been devoured by some wild beast.

He went to the place where he used to play as a boy and gathered things as children do nowadays and made images of clay or mud, such as men and women, and children, and birds, and other animals of all kinds, as though he wished that they might become live beings. He was greatly surprised that many of the things of adobe were soon gone and others were leaving, all alive and going off to some place to live. That is why there are all kinds of people, birds, and other animals in the world. In later years he became very great and fought all kinds of fierce beasts against the odds and overpowered them. He also calmed the wild winds and tempests, which power was given him by the sun. He is known as the first man.

I believe all this, just the same way the white men believe their stories. They don't look like the real, natural facts, but that is just the way it is. Some of these things are said about Jesus Christ, and people have written stories about him, but we cannot say for sure whether any of them happened. We can only know what we hear from other people. They say that if you tell this story you will bring a great storm of rain and wind, because the father eagle was coming down low to devour every living thing within reach.

So about two thousand of the Indians moved away in the latter part of February 1875, and in a few days they were camped on the East Verde River. Rations were running short, and some of the Tontos had been slowly moping around with baskets, singing and begging for coffee, sugar, and flour. One evening they came through in a hurry, nearly knocking somebody over. An Apache Yuma told them to go away, but they paid no attention to him and pointed arrows at him, threatening to shoot. After a while, someone told an older man that his son had been shot through the head but had not been seriously injured. The other Tontos got excited and came running with their guns, spoiling for a fight. The Apache Yumas and Apache Mojaves turned out, too, and met the Tontos. They were so close that they could almost touch each other. The whole two rows fired at the same time, and when the smoke cleared away there were about thirty-five Tontos lying on the ground. There were only about four

A memorial above Roosevelt Dam honoring Al Sieber (1844–1907), also known as Albert Sebers, the German-born chief of Indian scouts under Gen. George R. Crook during much of the fighting in Arizona.

people against them, and they wanted to keep on going, but the soldiers came up and stopped further fighting. When the Apache Yumas and Apache Mojaves returned to their camp they found some of their men wounded, as well as two white men. Everyone recovered. One of these white men was Al Sieber, the chief of scouts and a great Indian fighter, who was shot through the stomach. The other white man was shot through the side.

Sieber was lame for life. The other man, whose name I forget, was killed by an Indian named Justin Head, a returned student from the Indian School at Carlisle, Pennsylvania. Head was crazy to kill someone after he had been on a drunk for nearly two months, and one day he got his .30-30 and went to an Indian camp and began shooting. He killed a man and wounded a woman. When he got tired, he rode off to Camp Verde and went up to a group of Indians who were shelling corn. I had written a letter to one of them telling him that there was work at Mayer, but he didn't read English and the letter lay unopened for days. He went up to Justin Head and asked him to read the letter to him, but Justin Head answered, "I have killed Coholelah, your brother at Cottonwood, and now I'm going to kill you too." Justin shot the man through the head and then rode off. He caused more mayhem for a while, but then after a week he rode into Jerome and surrendered. He was taken to Prescott and tried for five murders. He got a life sentence at Florence State Penitentiary, but somehow he managed to get out and moved back to Pennsylvania, where he must have learned to be a bad man in the first place.

After all this trouble the Tontos were ordered to go ahead. The soldiers followed, then came the pack train, and after them the Yumas and Mojaves. The wounded who could not march were carried by the other Indians, while four medicine men marched alongside, two of them at a time, singing. The Tontos must have lost many of their people, because there was loud crying in their camp. The rations had been distributed, and everyone was hungry. So flour, sugar, and beef were sent to meet the Indians at the headwaters of Tonto Creek. Here several families left and went back to Four Peaks and the headwaters of Cave Creek. The main body, after a toilsome journey of about twenty days, at last reached their new home, which was in country unknown to them. There they were thrown among a lot of people they did not know, such as the Chiricahuas, the San Carlos, the Pinals, and the Cibecues, who probably were one tribe in the past but became separated just as the Yavapais had. They all have the same language, manners, songs, and religious ceremonies, the same style of dress, and the same kind of weapons, and when they meet for medicine dances, they follow the same procedures. It's just like Englishmen and Frenchmen. Anyway, we all look alike to white people.

A few days after their arrival, the chiefs of the Apache Mojaves and Apache Yumas were called to have a talk with the Indian agent and the commanding officer at San Carlos. They were told that because they were now at peace the Indians could not have firearms. They knew that some of the Indians had guns because they had posted a spy along the road from Globe to count anyone carrying weapons. Some of the young men decided to resist, saying that if they gave up their guns the soldiers would shoot them down. They had seen enough of that kind of treatment in the past. This is what the whites did to their kinfolk when they came to make a treaty at Skull Valley, at Camp Date Creek, and at Camp McDowell. Some of the young men said that they expected to be slaughtered at any minute.

The tribes were shown to the places in which they were to live. They stayed there for a long time, but in 1894 the Apache Yumas were allowed to go to Mohawk and Palomas, and in 1897 the Apache Mojaves went back to their old country near Camp Verde.

12

I will now return to my own life. I was brought to Fort Whipple by Captain Burns in 1873. His lieutenants were Thomas and Bishop. Dr. Washington Matthews always accompanied the command. After being there a few months the captain went away for some time, and when he returned he brought his wife, Annie Burns, and their little daughter, Katie. I nursed this girl and cared for her as I would for my own sister, and when Captain Burns bought her anything to wear, he would always buy me new clothing too.

One time, when he was away scouting, Mrs. Burns gave me ten dollars to buy a pair of shoes, since I ran around barefoot. I didn't mind, for I had never had anything to wear on my feet, and, in fact, when I was very small, I ran around altogether naked. But now I was living a different life, and I had to dress myself somewhat decently. So one fine morning when the officers' ambulance was going to Prescott, I went with it, holding the ten-dollar bill tightly in my hand. When we got to town, the driver showed me where there was a shoe shop. I went and told them what I wanted, and the clerk showed me a fine pair of boots, shiny and bright. They were so pretty that I was afraid he was going to take them away. I gave the man my ten dollars and left without waiting for any change. When we got back to the fort, I went around to the back of the house, since I did not want Mrs. Burns to see the boots for fear she might say they were not the right kind or did not fit me. But she asked me what I had bought. I showed her the bundle, and she told me to put the boots on my feet. I put them on and walked proudly up to her in my fancy-looking boots. I soon noticed that she was not in good humor, as she usually was, when she saw the size of the boots. They were size 7, and I wore size 4. She did not like them, but I didn't care, even if they were three sizes too large. She was thinking about that ten-dollar bill, and the next morning she gave me a note to take to Prescott. I didn't want to lose any time waiting for the ambulance, so I ran all the way and handed the man the note.

He gave me $2.50, and I ran back and gave Mrs. Burns the change. I wore the boots all of the time, but they were so big that they turned up over the ends of my feet. Mrs. Burns said, "You have got fine-looking boots now. I tried to make you understand that they were too large for you, but you were anxious for them, so you must wear them off your hide." She never bought me anything more, but she used me as one of her own children in doing chores.

Captain Burns returned to the post sick, after having been out scouting for the Hualapais. When his command returned, he was put on the sick list the whole winter. Dr. Matthews attended to him, and Lieutenant Ross, an infantry officer, called on him frequently to keep him company. All this seemed to do Captain Burns no good, so he was finally advised to go to Washington, D.C. They supposed that Captain Burns's parents lived there, but they really lived in Ireland, and he used to tell me that he was going to take me to their home one day. I thought this would really happen, and that I would never see Arizona again to see my people and be in my homeland.

At last Captain Burns got a sick leave, a leave of absence, and started in a government wagon overland to Kansas, where he was to take a train. He was going to have to pass through some rough country—Arizona, New Mexico, Colorado, and Kansas. He was attended by Dr. William H. Corbusier and an escort of six soldiers, and Mrs. Burns and the two children went with him. Before he left Fort Whipple, he bought me a new suit of clothes and left instructions with Lieutenant H. S. Bishop to take good care of his Apache mickie, which means child in Irish. The suit at first was a good fit, but before long the pants were halfway up my legs and the vest halfway up my back. I looked just as you would expect an orphan child to look. Lieutenant Bishop took me to the company tailor and told him to measure me for a suit of navy blue cloth that could not be torn easily, since I wore out my clothes very fast, especially the pants at the knees.

Every payday the soldiers would put in some money and give it to Sergeant Hanlon, who would buy me shirts, candy, and other things that I foolishly wanted. I was a kind of pet of G Troop and was treated very well by the officers and men.

William H. Corbusier, an army doctor who befriended Mike Burns and helped him draft portions of his memoir.

One day a private from A Troop, which was stationed at Camp Verde, was up at Fort Whipple escorting the paymaster, Major Stanley of the Department of Arizona. The post had just finished building a reservoir, on a hill south of the post, and General Crook had the 23rd Infantry band play at the dedication. The private was out gambling or drinking, I'm not sure which, and he was supposed to go home, but it was late at night and he couldn't see where he was going. He strayed off the path and wound up at the reservoir, which was next to a big building where the controls were housed. The post provost sergeant was supposed to lock the doors at night, but somehow he hadn't, and this man fell into the reservoir, which was about thirty feet deep. It was midwinter, and the guards who were supposed to check the reservoir hadn't left the guardhouse. They didn't hear the man yell when he fell in. When the provost sergeant went to unlock the reservoir the next day he found the man floating in the water, drowned. Some soldiers fished him out, and the private from Camp Verde was buried that afternoon.

I lived with Lieutenant Bishop at Fort Whipple. One day I was alone on the front porch of the soldiers' quarters when about half a dozen Hualapai scouts came up. They had been hunting Apaches, and they were about to receive their discharges from the service. One of them said, "I would like to see this lad out in the hills. I would use him up this way." The first thing I knew, he had grabbed me by the throat and pushed me up against a post. I gave a big yell, and Sergeant Hanlon rushed out and hit the Indian on the jaw with his fist. He kicked him off the porch and made the rest of the scouts move on. When I came to, my throat was almost closed and my eyes were full of tears. I saw those Indians run to their camp. They looked behind them at times, but they kept going, and I never saw them again—nor did I care to see them again, either.

A few months later a party of soldiers came in with two girls and three boys. The girls were wounded, and they were kept apart from the others in a tent. They were guarded, but all the same they went missing. One of the girls had had her arm cut off, since her wound was close to her shoulder joint, and even though the doctor had done a good job they decided that they wanted to go home, somewhere in the mountains behind Squaw Peak. The boys stayed at the fort for nearly two years, until all the Indians were gathered at Camp Verde. Then the boys were taken home to their relatives.

If they had stayed, they could have learned how to speak English. At that time I was asked if I did not want to return to my people, but I went on with my business as if I had not heard, since I was satisfied where I was. I had no relatives living, for they had all been killed at the caves on the Salt River, and I would have been lost among the Indians. Was there any use of my going back to them just because they were Indians and so was I? I had a good house to stay in, a good bed, plenty of blankets, plenty to eat, and only a little work to do. I didn't need anything. Life was comfortable. What more could anybody want? I'd like to know.

Every Sunday, half a dozen soldiers would go out on passes to hunt rabbits. They had two greyhounds that had belonged to Captain Burns, and he had given me a nice little sorrel pony that I would ride along with the crowd. We would come back with twenty-five or thirty jackrabbits, a mess for the whole company. We had all kinds of good times and sports.

After a time, two soldiers who had gone with Captain Burns returned with the news of his death, and I cried all day and all night, just the same as if I had lost a father. He died after crossing the Little Colorado River at Navajo Spring. I am not certain about the day and month. His body was taken to Fort Wingate, New Mexico, and buried there. Mrs. Burns and the children continued their journey to Washington, where her father and mother lived. I had never learned her maiden name and so had no idea of how to contact her.

I learned the name later from Captain John G. Bourke, of the Third Cavalry, who was an aide-de-camp to General Crook. He once gave me a whipping because I said some swearwords. I didn't know what I was saying, but Captain Bourke said that they were no words for a boy to use, so he punished me for them. I have remembered all this time and never repeated them. I've been talking for a long time without using swearwords, and so could everybody if they wanted to.

Captain Bourke later told me that Mrs. Burns had died in Washington, and he advised me to write to her parents to say that Captain Burns had adopted me and I was one of their family. In that way, he said, one day I would have a share of their property. But he forgot to give me their address, and all I knew was that they were in Washington and had a lot of valuable property, all to be given to the two Burns children. In those days I didn't know a thing about the law, and I lost out. Instead of being a wealthy man, I now live in poverty.

I want to say a little more about Captain Bourke, who has written much about the life of General Crook and the campaigns against the Apaches in his book *On the Border with Crook*. I helped him with much of what he wrote, and he promised that when the book was finished and selling I would get a share of the money. I went to a lot of trouble to talk with old Indians about how they used to live, and the kinds of things they used to eat before the white man's food, such as flour, sugar, coffee, beans, and potatoes, came into general use among the Indians. I learned that the principal food was mescal, which could be gathered at any season. All you have to do is dig one out and cut it into a shape like a cabbage, and then dig a pit about three or four feet deep and six or eight feet wide. Then you build a

An elderly Kwevkepaya couple in their high-desert camp.

fire so that the whole pit becomes like a furnace, and then you bake the mescal. Some people call the mescal "century plant," but I don't really believe it lives a century. Instead, it puts out a flower, and then after a couple of years it just dries up and falls over.

There are many other plants that are good to eat, but these ripen at different times of the year. Squawberries open in May. Next is the water cactus, then the paloverde trees, and then the joint cactus, which turns red and opens out; its meaty parts and black seeds are very sweet. The juice is very strong, and also sweet. The Indians go out with burden baskets and small poles and drag the fruit off these cacti like ripe pears. They let the fruit dry in the sun a little, but it doesn't last long; when rain gets on it, it melts away and vanishes. The people also make flour of the mesquite beans that they go and gather, drying them on the ground. Then there's the prickly pear, which the Mexicans call *tuna*. The pears are red but thorny, and you have to use something like a blacksmith's tongs to get at them. But in the old days the women would just take a handful of brush and then drag it back and forth over the fruit until all the thorns were pulled off. You can dry these like peaches or apples, and they will keep for months or years in a dry place.

Then there are the acorns that grow on oak trees, and walnuts, which ripen at the same time. Later in fall the wild sunflower ripens, and other plants too. The scrub pine, or piñon, has many seeds, though it takes a lot of work to get at them. There are still more foods too numerous to write about.

I have often told people that Indians had more to eat in the old days than they do now. It seems that civilization has destroyed the old ways, since their places are no longer theirs; everywhere the Indians go, all the lands have been fenced and some white man has enclosed all the trees.

I learned long afterward that Captain Bourke had died at San Antonio, Texas, and I heard nothing more about the money from his book *On the Border with Crook*.

13

In July 1875, the Fifth Cavalry was ordered east, to be replaced by the Sixth Cavalry. My old friend Lieutenant Bishop went to see General Crook about taking me with him. The good-hearted general consented, telling Bishop to be sure that he and the company took good care of me.

We started from Fort Whipple on July 1. It took three days to get to Camp Verde. We stayed at the fort the next day, July 4, until so many of the men got drunk that, in the afternoon, the lieutenant ordered the company to move some distance outside the post. That night eight or ten of the men deserted, my old friend Sergeant Hanlon among them. They probably liked the climate of Arizona better than any other climate. Lieutenant Bishop didn't seem concerned. We marched to the headwaters of Beaver Creek and made our next camp. It took all day to get to the next waterhole, where we made camp far down in a canyon. At dawn we climbed up to a divide, and there I gazed at the rising sun and could see the hills and ranges sloping far away toward Four Peaks. I cried and said to myself, "Good-bye my homeland, and water, and trees and rocks. There is no chance that I shall live long enough to come back to this land." I had no living relatives at all, and I made up my mind to try to forget my people and country. Anyone who has had to live by himself in the world knows what it is like to have no one to help when he is in need. Hopeless, I resolved to go with the white people and learn their ways.

We marched along a valley where there was a small stream of water and fine green cottonwood trees and willows, and there we made camp. That evening I was attacked with chills and fever, and Lieutenant Bishop gave me some medicine and rolled me up in blankets. I sweated under the thick covers all night, and the next morning I was better and was able to eat. We started again and passed the place where Apaches had shot Lieutenant Charles King two years before.

With his arm broken, he lay under a cedar tree unconscious, exposed to enemy fire. His sergeant, a man named Logan, ran back to camp to get more soldiers. Seven Apache Yuma scouts posted themselves and shot at the enemy to hold them back. If they had not been there King would have been killed. When a company of soldiers arrived they forced the seven scouts to go ahead of them, threatening to shoot them if they didn't obey. When King came to, he declared that Sergeant Logan had saved his life, though the credit really belonged to the Apache Yumas. But that's the way it always is: the Indians are left behind.

From the spot where Lieutenant King was wounded, we went down to the Little Colorado River, which was very high and hard to cross, and we camped on the far side. The next day we made five or six miles before meeting up with a troop of the Sixth Cavalry. The troop was going to take our place at Fort Whipple, and we expected to change horses with them, but found that they had already done so with the other troops they had met. The horses used by the Fifth Cavalry were small Mexican or California ones and could travel over the rough country much better than the large horses, which were good on level ground, and they could live on most any kind of weed or scrub and even sunflowers and oak brush, just like jack mules.

We stayed in camp for a day while the men shot at targets as a way of saluting the soldiers who were to take their place. We then moved on to Navajo Springs. On the surface, all around, were the skeletons of dead animals. There was a doctor in the troop, and he went too close to the muddy springs and stepped onto ground that he thought was dry. Fortunately, someone saw him sink into the mud clear up to his shoulders. Several soldiers pulled him out with a rope and scraped the mud off him with a knife. He had a nice gold watch, but it didn't look so nice after that, and finally it stopped running. The doctor never used it again.

We came to a crystal-clear spring the next day, and everybody enjoyed drinking from it. Nearby we found a Navajo village that had plenty of milk and cheese to sell, which they got from sheep and goats. They had no cattle. I stayed away from the Indians. Some of them could speak the Apache language, but only that of the White Mountain Apaches, of which I could make out only a few words, and I could not understand one of the men who was trying to ask me questions about who I was. Some of the soldiers said that the Navajos were going to take me back to their camp and keep me, so I hid in a corner of Lieutenant Bishop's tent. He laughed at me and asked me what was happening, but I didn't answer, since I was afraid that the Indians would hear my voice.

The evening came, and the Indians left our camp to go home. Pretty soon the soldiers grabbed their guns and started running toward a great rocky canyon. There was an old Irishman in the company named Tom Broderick who could not read or write but who was a jolly fellow. It seems that he had gone out to hunt rabbits and had strayed deep into this canyon. He began to sing an old Irish song, and an echo came back to him. He stopped, and then he started singing again, and the echo came back to him again. This frightened him. He thought that Apaches were on the hillsides howling to others that he was coming. He turned around and ran back to camp, bareheaded, and breathlessly told the others that Apaches were after him. The men turned out and went to the canyon with Tom, where they found his hat. He showed them where he had heard the yelling coming from. Some of the soldiers were talking, and their echo came back. When they understood what Tom had been hearing, they made fun of him and called him a babe in the woods.

This place had a few little cornfields, watered by a little stream that flowed white because of all the white clay in the hills. The soldiers had to put cactus heads in their coffee to settle the white color down, but it looked like milk, and so the soldiers drank it. The company followed this little stream eastward and made another camp.

The next day soldiers from Fort Wingate, New Mexico, came out to meet us. The company went on to the fort. A few days later, Lieutenant Bishop took me to the soldiers' graveyard and showed me where Captain Burns had been laid to rest. When I saw his grave I couldn't help shedding tears, because when he was alive he treated me as if I were his own child, saying, when he left Fort Whipple, "My boy, you'll be all right. I'll return in a short time, and then we'll leave for Ireland, my father's home."

Lieutenant Bishop said to me, "This is the only way that we see our old friends." Several men of the company went to the grave and fired a salute over it.

We were at Fort Wingate for more than a month. Lieutenant

Bishop had orders to remain until the arrival of four companies from Fort Apache, Fort Thomas, and the San Carlos Agency. After they arrived we resumed our march, and in a few days came to another Indian village, whether Navajo or Zuni or Pueblo I could not say. The lieutenant bought five sheep from the Indians, paying three dollars apiece, so the company had fresh meat that night.

I do not recollect much about the journey to Pueblo, New Mexico, except that the Rio Grande was very high, and we could not ford it at the crossing. There was a ferry there, with a crew of Pueblo Indians pulling a great coil of rope. It took them all day to ferry the wagons, horses, and soldiers across. We reached Albuquerque late that night and found that there was a dance going on. It was a pretty rough Mexican town. The soldiers went off to take in the scene, and soon some of them got into a fray. One soldier was killed, as were three Mexicans.

Early the next morning we followed the banks of the Rio Grande and camped about fifteen miles above Albuquerque. We then moved on to a Pueblo Indian village where the Indians had farms and peach trees, and they sold food to the soldiers. In two days we reached Santa Fe, and another five took us to Fort Union. There were several companies of the Fifth and the Sixth Cavalry in camp there. At that place Colonel Wesley Merritt, the new commander, joined us, as did the new captain for G Troop, Edward M. Hayes. Bishop, being only a second lieutenant, had to fall back. Lieutenant Thomas was a first lieutenant, but he was on staff duty at headquarters with General Crook. The whole command had to change horses. Lieutenant Bishop didn't want to give up his little horse, Maude. She was small, but she could travel farther than any of the big horses. I did not want to give up my little sorrel, and I asked him to see whether we could keep our mounts. He was told that he'd have to buy them at the price the government paid, so he bought them.

After we left Fort Union we came to a town called Trinidad, and then in a few more days to Fort Lyon, Colorado. Here Colonel Merritt ordered the different companies to their various stations. C and G Troops were sent to Camp Supply, in the Indian Territory, about ninety-five miles away. The rest of the soldiers went on to Fort Riley, Kansas, by train.

I saw my first locomotive at Fort Lyon, and I was anxious to ride in the cars, but the company I was with was going overland to their station. We marched down the Arkansas River and in about a week arrived at Fort Dodge, and two of the companies that were to be stationed there gave a dance with lots of drinks, such as whiskey, beer, and cider. Lieutenant Bishop remained here until some recruits for C and G Troops arrived on the train. He told the new men to be ready to leave at 6:00 a.m. sharp, and then the next morning we crossed the river at sunup and went the same way as the command that had gone ahead. The country was flat, with no hills or mountains, only the level plain covered with buffalo grass, short and fine as feathers.

When we were about three days out, and on the last day's march to Camp Supply, Lieutenant Bishop invited me to ride with him away from the main road. He pointed out some whitish animals to me that I thought were goats, but he said they were antelopes and said he would get some fresh meat. So he got off his horse, handed me the bridle, went down on his knees, and crawled until he got within rifle shot, about three or four hundred yards away, when he fired at them, but none fell. One acted sort of weak, though. I took his horse to him, and he said that he had wounded one and that it would soon be dead. We went after it on a run, but I could not keep up with him. I had a gun in my hands and did not have hold of the reins, and going down a grade the pony I was riding fell and rolled over on his back. One of my legs was caught under the pony. Lieutenant Bishop, looking back, saw the pony's legs sticking straight up in the air, turned back, and pulled the horse off me. He tried to help me, but my leg was almost mashed. He said the only way to fix it was to straighten it out, and when he pulled on my leg it hurt so much that I cried. Lieutenant Bishop told me to stay there and went to get the light wagon. He came back shortly with several of the men, spread a blanket, laid me on it, and put me in the wagon along with the broken saddle. The horse wasn't hurt. We reached Camp Supply toward evening, and I had to stay in the hospital for nearly three months. At last I was strong enough to go back to Lieutenant Bishop.

It was good country for game, such as prairie chicken, wild turkeys, and buffalo. Some of the men in the company used to go out in their wagons for three or four days down Beaver Creek and the Canadian River and come back loaded down with meat. They told me that I ought to go out a few miles and kill a few for myself. So one evening I got a shotgun and some shells and went out to a grove of big cottonwood trees and spied what I thought were two turkeys. I went up to them and blasted away, and put them in a big sack and carried it back to camp, proud to be a big hunter. I knew the officers would be pleased to feast on such fine birds, and I was boarding at the same mess they were, so I took them to the kitchen and threw the sack down, tired from carrying it. I went to my room to go to sleep but was too excited, so I went back to the kitchen, anxious to see the turkeys dressed and ready to cook. When I got there I found my sack lying outside, and when I went into the kitchen the cook was not in a good mood. He told me to take those two stinking buzzards clear away from there, since buzzards aren't fit to eat. I took the birds out of the sack, and sure enough they were buzzards. I'd carried them for ten miles, those heavy stinking buzzards, and all for nothing.

The prairie often caught fire around Camp Supply, and the soldiers were often called out to fight fires with wet grain sacks. There was once a fire on the other side of Beaver Creek from the post, set by Indians who had driven off some cattle and were burning the prairie to cover their tracks. The post scout, a man named Frank Grouard—a noted Indian fighter who had an Indian wife and who knew every foot of the plains just as well as any Plains Indian did—was dispatched to go out with Lieutenant Bishop to the ranch where the cattle had come from. Lieutenant Bishop told me not to sleep, since we would soon be on the march. I was able by now to carry a gun, so we strapped guns and ammunition to our saddles and mounted up. We arrived at the ranch toward morning, and two cowboys joined us and showed us where the Indians had driven off the cattle. We went on some distance and found three butchered cows with only the best parts taken. They must have had seventy-five or a hundred head, because we could see their trail even through the burned grass.

The cowboys said that it had been about four days since they missed the cattle, and the grass was still burning. We rode for three days and came to the Seminole River. Smoke was coming up on the other side of the river, and soon we came to a place where the fire finally stopped beyond the bottomlands. It looked as if the Indians had separated, taking part of the herd elsewhere. Lieutenant Bishop told us to be ready to fight, since Indians might be near. We went about ten miles and saw some ponies, which the lieutenant ordered some of the men to capture. They rode out, and all at once a volley of shots rang out. The soldiers ducked behind their horses and rode into a huge Indian camp. When I followed I saw some Indian women and children outside a tepee, and two dead men on the ground, one an Indian and one a soldier. There was a letter lying next to the dead Indian.

Leaving before the Indians could counterattack, we took the women and children, thirteen of them, captive, and went back through a thick fog thirty-five miles or so to the Seminole River, driving a herd of about two hundred ponies with us. We made camp in the river bottom, digging holes in the sand for shelter in case we were attacked. A couple of the old Indian women howled all night long, hoping that some of the young braves had followed us and would find them. We spent the night unharmed, though, and crossed the river the next morning, meeting up with twenty-five or thirty reinforcements. We all reached Camp Supply toward evening. I showed Lieutenant Bishop a nice pair of ponies, and he said I could get them once we settled down.

The Indians we attacked were Seminoles, out on a hunt, who had joined up with the Sac and Fox people. They had been making raids south from Nebraska down into Kansas and the Indian Territory. Their chief actually had a pass to hunt buffalo, but they must have fallen in with a bad set of Sac and Fox Indians and gotten into trouble. This was somewhere between April 22 and April 27, 1876.

We put the prisoners and ponies into the hands of the military authorities; we heard later that the prisoners would be sent to Fort Reno or the Darlington Agency, out in the Indian Territory. The commanding officer ordered that nothing be taken from the prisoners, and Lieutenant Bishop asked me how I felt about that order. We had only one man killed but had killed three Indians, and we could have ransacked the camp but didn't. I really expected those two pretty little ponies for my service, at the risk of my life, but the ponies had to go to Fort Reno with the Indians.

Frank Grouard took the prisoners and the ponies away. All my hope was in vain, and I got nothing. This was close on the start of spring out there, and it was then that we heard that there was a war going on up north between General Crook and the Sioux Indians. Their chief's name was Sitting Bull, but he was really a subchief and medicine man. The real chiefs were Spotted Tail and Red Cloud, and old Standing Bear at the Standing Rock Agency, and many others.

General Crook sent for the Fifth Cavalry to help him up there. He had had several fights with the Sioux in the Big Horn Mountains and at the headwaters of the Tongue River. In one of them General Crook ordered his men to pull back, leaving the dead and wounded on the battlefield, instead of pursuing the Indians, who appeared to be falling back, too. Some of the junior officers complained to the War Department in Washington that he should be tried for cowardice. The general answered that the Indians were luring them into a trap; he said he had gone up against all kinds of Indians and knew how they fought. Some investigators went out from Washington and looked the battlefield over, and they found a rough gulch with a bunch of dug holes on the banks behind some big rocks, just right for a person to sit behind and shoot from. It was that way for at least a mile, and any trooper would have had to dismount and lead his horse through this little canyon. The command would have been slaughtered, just like General Custer's.

The young officers would have gone right into that trap, and the Indians under Crazy Horse and Roman Nose and Rain in the Face would have whipped them. These Indians were not like Apaches: there were a lot of them, and they had lots of rifles and ammunition. The Apaches had bows and arrows and couldn't fight on rainy days, since the string on their bows would come apart if it got wet. They had just a few flintlocks. They had many disadvantages when it came to war.

In early May 1876, Captain Jacob Adams, who was the commanding officer of C Troop and of Camp Supply, received orders from headquarters to pull up and join General Crook up at Fort D. A. Russell, in Wyoming. Lieutenant Bishop said that we must go together, and so I went along as a volunteer scout, even though I didn't have a horse. Lieutenant Bishop said that I would get one up north.

That was the first time I ever rode on a railroad train. We went from Fort Lyon to Denver and then north. I rode on the top of one of the cars with the soldiers, and we had a great time shooting at deer and antelope on the way. The bullets struck the ground a long way ahead of the animals, all, I learned later, on account of the train's going much faster than a normal train did, for this was a special train ordered to get us up to Cheyenne as soon as possible. I enjoyed the scenery for a while, the mountains and the prairies, and then tied a strap around my waist and went to sleep. When I awoke I found that I had rolled over and was hanging over the edge of the car, held only by the strap. I slid down onto the car rim, and the strap was all that kept me alive, and then I woke up and found out where I was, and I got on my feet again. The Great Omniscient was around and had given me the hand of life.

Finally the train reached Cheyenne, where General Merritt was waiting for us, and we marched to Fort D. A. Russell, three miles from there. We waited there for a few days for new mounts. Only a few arrived, enough for General Merritt to take up into the Black Hills, so I still had no horse to ride. Lieutenant Bishop made arrangements with the quartermaster for me to ride in a wagon with a light load. I crawled into one of the grain wagons and we started off. All at once I heard a kind of crack and felt the wagon start rolling down a steep gulch, and sacks of grain rolled over on top of me. I screamed for help and fought for breath until the soldiers who were escorting the wagons cut the canvas sides and pulled me out by my arms. It would have been hard luck for me if I had not fallen on the flat of my stomach, but I was not injured.

On the third day we arrived at Fort Laramie, where we found General Merritt—the men called him General Merritt because he had been a general in the Civil War between the North and the South, but he was really a colonel, promoted in 1875—and other officers. Our scouts were Frank Grouard and Bill Cody, along with many other men who had been with these two old scouts for years. Buffalo Bill was an all-around good shot with a pistol and rifle, on foot or on horseback. I don't know about Frank Grouard as a shot. Oh, yes— out on the plains in those days was Wild Bill Hickock, with his long hair and buckskin shirt, who was said not to have ever been beaten in pistol shooting, and he was a good shot with a gun too. A coward killed Wild Bill at Deadwood, walked up to him while he was playing faro, and shot him through the back and instantly killed him. No one knew anything about the man, but many said that if he had walked up to Wild Bill with a gun in his hand, Wild Bill would have got him first. The man who killed Wild Bill, it's said, did so because Wild Bill killed some relative of his at a saloon in Cheyenne. Wild Bill was a desperado, but he would not do anything cowardly. This must have been in 1879.

Buffalo Bill and Frank Grouard were good scouts and trustworthy people. I don't know whether they killed anyone, but they took the officers through Indian country. Many of them had lived with Indians in order to learn their ways and languages, and they were of much help to the government.

The Fifth Cavalry arrived at Fort Laramie in the middle of May. Finally more horses came, and a few days later the command started north toward the Black Hills. General Merritt received a telegram with orders to go up into the foothills and valleys between Fort Laramie and the Black Hills to cut off small parties of Indians who were escaping from their reservations to go out on the warpath and join up with Sitting Bull up north.

The first day out, we camped at a place with a little creek called Hack Creek. I was riding with the rear guard, talking with one of the old soldiers about ways to endure the hardships of scouting, when he gave me a chew of tobacco, telling me that all scouts and soldiers used it to ward off thirst and hunger and to feel strong. At the first taste I wanted to throw it out of my mouth, but I was afraid that the man would scold me, since we were out in the wild country where there was no place to buy any more tobacco. I kept it in my mouth for three or four hours before finally spitting it out. I could hardly speak with the taste of that strong tobacco in my mouth, and I could only motion for water, but I didn't dare use much of it since we were traveling through unknown country. I didn't say a word until we reached camp. When we rode in, I was so sick that I rolled off my horse and fell to the ground. Lieutenant Bishop asked me who had given me whiskey. I shook my head, so he thought I was drunk. He spread a blanket on the ground for me to lie on. I lay there until evening, and when supper was ready Lieutenant Bishop called me, but I didn't want to eat. I vomited all night and still wasn't hungry the next morning, and he told me to go to the doctor, but I said that I would be all right in a few days.

_14_

On the next march we reached Sage Creek, about halfway between the Black Hills and Fort Laramie. Here General Merritt received a message from headquarters at Fort Omaha, Nebraska, saying that it had been reported that the Sioux had left their reservation and were going north to join Sitting Bull in the Big Horn Mountains. Sitting Bull, a great medicine man and talker, was the head of all the war chiefs—among them Crazy Horse, Standing Bear, Lone Star, Rain in the Face, and Old Man Afraid of His Horses. The Sioux tribe numbered about sixty thousand souls, scattered across seven different agencies.

He sent an orderly around the camps to say that we would be moving early to a camp called Crazy Woman's Forks. The command went down to a dry creek and made camp, and the soldiers had to dig for water since the surface water was thick with a kind of whitish clay mud, and even the horses would not drink it. The next day the command moved down the valley to a nice green cottonwood bottomland, with clear running water.

At every camp men were sent out on the hills with signal flags, some with a white square in the center, others with a black square. One morning these pickets signaled that about thirty Indians were coming right into the camp from the east. Some fool was right out in the open, in sight of the Indians, because the Indians understood the signal and hurriedly retreated in the direction from which they had come, over by the Red Cloud Agency. Some soldiers and scouts under Buffalo Bill went after them, and they had a running fight, but I cannot tell who had the better of it that day. The scouts and soldiers returned that night with their horses all tired out, and they were tired, too, saying that they had never even seen any Indians to shoot.

The command stayed in camp the next day, while some scouts went north toward the Black Hills to see whether they could spot any

Indian trails. They said that they could see no trails either coming or going, so the next day the command moved camp toward the Red Cloud Agency at a place called Cottonwood Flat. The camp posted pickets on the hills. Before long horsemen came toward the camp from a distance of about four miles. Buffalo Bill and his scouts, who were up above the canyon where the camp was, signaled when the horsemen got within two miles, but Buffalo Bill saw that the pickets would be right in the way of the approaching Indians and that he and his men were too far away to save them. Buffalo Bill took out his long-range .50 caliber rifle. Five mounted Indians were closing up, and three more were on foot. One of the mounted Indians had a great feather war bonnet, so he must have been a chief. Buffalo Bill took aim at him from a mile away and shot, and when the smoke cleared he saw that he had hit the Indian's horse. With the next shot he brought his man down. The rest of the Indians scattered.

When Buffalo Bill and Frank Grouard got to where the man lay, they quickly recognized him as a young Cheyenne chief from Fort Robinson, Nebraska. The party was going off to join Sitting Bull at the headwaters of the Yellowstone River. Buffalo Bill took almost everything belonging to the Indian he had just killed. Probably this was not the only Indian he had ever killed, either. It's supposed that he killed almost everything he shot.

He was called Buffalo Bill, but his real name was Bill Cody. His home was on the Platte River about eighteen miles below Fort McPherson, Nebraska. I once went to an exhibition of his shooting at North Platte, Nebraska, about twenty-four miles from the fort. I saw him shoot a small apple off a girl's head while he had his back turned, looking at a looking glass over his shoulder. He must have had a very steady hand. Whoever gets shot at that way has to be a brave person, and probably well paid, too.

Then there was Buffalo Chip. He probably got his name from gathering buffalo manure or dung to build a fire when he was a boy working for Buffalo Bill. That was used for fuel out there on the tree-less plains. There are some books that say that Buffalo Chip was once up a tree without a rifle while three bears were chasing him, and they circled round and round the tree, and Buffalo Chip killed one with his pistol. Then Buffalo Bill came up fast on his horse and shot the other two fierce bears. These books were written by other people, so much of what is written about Buffalo Bill, Frank Grouard, and Wild Bill is exaggerated. You never hear about what other people besides themselves were doing at the time.

But back to Buffalo Bill. There were a good many Cheyenne Indians and Arapahos among the Sioux in Nebraska, Dakota, and the Wyoming Territory. Buffalo Bill made short work of that one and saved two innocent soldiers.

On reaching Sage Creek that evening, the officers were told to go to General Merritt's headquarters. There they were given the news that General Custer and all his men had been killed by the Sioux up in the foothills of the Big Horn Mountains. General Merritt had orders to proceed north to join General Crook's command on Goose Creek, at the headwaters of the Tongue River. This was on the last day of July.

The next day we pulled out on the road toward the Big Horns. We met two men on foot who told us that they were originally seven in number. They had started away from the Big Horn Mountains and crossed the Powder River, then made camp; early the next morning sixty-five or seventy-five Indians attacked them. Two men were killed right then. The rest of the men got under their wagon and dug out a trench. Two got shot through the head, but the other two kept shooting until the Indians went away. They had been on the road for four days since then. General Merritt selected three companies under Major Upham to escort the two men back to the site, planning to rendezvous at the Powder River. The next day, the general sent out two more companies to go scouting, and everyone in the command wanted to volunteer to go shoot Indians. General Merritt said there would be plenty of time for all that.

A few days later we came to Fort Phil Kearney, which the government had abandoned a few years earlier. There was a nice clear stream flowing near the fort, emptying into the Yellowstone, and we could see plenty of trout, small and large, in it. It must have been a fine fishing spot for the soldiers, and here our command rested. The water was better than that of the Powder River, which was muddy. I started to unsaddle my horse when I noticed that Lieutenant Bishop was laughing, and that none of the soldiers had unsaddled their horses yet. Instead, we ate lunch and pushed on into the mountains, climbing for a long time through the night before stopping early in the morning to make camp until daylight. When the sun came we ate breakfast, and it was the first time since leaving Fort Fetterman that bugle calls were sounded. The regimental flag was raised over General Merritt's camp, and then the bugle sounded the order for us to march out in twos. We rode fifteen miles to General Crook's camp, with its large command of soldiers, civilians, packers and teamsters, and Indian scouts, about 2,700 men in all. General Merritt added the ten companies of his regiment, another 850 men.

Lieutenant Bishop said that he would see to it that I would be carried on the rolls as a volunteer Indian scout of the Fifth US Cavalry, so that I could draw rations and be given an allowance of horse feed. We soon received orders to get ready to march the next morning and to draw fifteen days' rations, so Lieutenant Bishop went over to the commissary to make sure that I would be taken care of. I can't say for sure what day of the month this was, or even what month. I was not educated in those days, and you must remember that I had spent only four years in civilization and could speak only enough English to get by. This must have been in the year 1876, and, I think, the early part of August.

The next day we set off. Ten men from each company stayed behind, putting all the team horses and mules into a great corral made of wagons, which would provide defense in case Indians attacked. We left all our blankets and tents behind. There were several cavalry regiments, and great strings of infantry. Someone said that there must have been seventy-five companies in the command, enough to sweep away all the Indians in the Northwest. An old soldier said, "Oh, no. You can boast all you want about this great array of soldiers, but that wouldn't scare old Sitting Bull." He went on to tell a story about being at the Standing Rock Agency with seven companies, which Sitting Bull attacked, charging in and shooting right and left. The soldiers hid in the post, and the Indians retreated because most of them had spears and bows and arrows and couldn't shoot through the wooden fortifications. The old soldier said, "I have put in five years in the Seventh Cavalry, all through the Indian Territory, Texas, and Kansas, fighting Cheyenne, Arapahos, Seminoles, Pawnees, Kiowas, Lipan Apaches, and Comanches. The Comanches were the only ones to put up much of a fight, and they were the finest horsemen on the plains, and they won't miss you, either. But these Sioux are brave fighters; they always meet you and hardly ever turn away and run. They always travel in great numbers, at least five hundred, scouring the country for enemies to surround and kill."

The young recruits listened attentively to the old soldier, and I suppose they were wondering about whether they would come into such close quarters with the Indians. He told them that the Indians always fight on horseback; you never see them fight on the ground. So he said that because it was hard to aim well on horseback, the soldiers should drop to the ground and take careful aim when they fight the Sioux.

I met up with General Crook, whose Apache Mojave name means "old woman's eyes." Lieutenant Bishop took me to see him, and General Crook recognized me at once. "Well, well," he said. "Here is that Apache boy Mickie Burns. And how are you, Mickie? Are you lost, being so far away from home?"

"I have no home, sir," I replied. "My home is just where I make my bed."

"That is true, my boy," the general said. "I had forgotten that your parents were killed at the Salt River caves." He added that it had to be done, otherwise there would still be fighting there today. Then he said, "My boy Mickie, forget about the past and resolve to do the best you can. You will be a great soldier when you grow up. Listen to Lieutenant Bishop's advice. He will never lead you wrong."

General Crook was fond of Lieutenant Bishop, and he knew that he was a brave young man. He kept him from being dishonorably dismissed from the army, instead giving him three months' confinement to his room when Lieutenant Bishop shot a butcher on the road to Fort Whipple. The civilian court in Prescott fined the lieutenant five hundred dollars, and he was supposed to be a free man, but the authorities at Fort Whipple court-martialed him for conduct unbecoming an officer. General Crook rejected the sentence.

The next morning we pulled out and marched down the Powder River, down where General Crook had fought a skirmish earlier with about 1,500 Indians. Then we came to another battleground from the preceding winter, where General Crook had ordered a charge uphill that fell apart when the commanding officer was shot and the men started running away. The Indians fired at the retreating soldiers. Nearly the whole company was killed—it is reported that only two or three men were left alive. General Crook got the worst of this fight against about 3,500 of Sitting Bull's warriors. But it could have been worse still if he had followed his young officers' advice and sent the whole command charging up that hill, where Sitting Bull had laid a very careful trap. General Crook knew how the Indians fight.

The command marched on, traveling by night with orders not to smoke, the column so tight that the horses knocked against one another's heels. At daylight, near the Tongue River, we passed a mound of Indian petroglyphs, with pictures of Indians, white men, animals, and battles. This was somewhere near Little Rose Bud Creek, where we met up with another column of soldiers commanded by General Terry, the head of the whole Department of the North. He had seven companies of Custer's command—the other five companies had been slaughtered—in the Seventh Cavalry, plus the First Cavalry, plus the Ninth and Tenth Cavalries, the last of which were black men.

I suppose that Terry and Crook had a great talk about the Sioux War and pursuing the trail of Sitting Bull, and the next day General Crook announced that we were to follow it and capture the chief. There must have been eight thousand soldiers in the command, with General Terry as the ranking officer. We passed across the mountains for a few miles, then down into the canyons back toward the Tongue River, where we made camp where Sitting Bull had made his not long before. When the companies called roll it was discovered that two men were missing, and the next day they were found lying side by side shot right through their heads. We supposed that the two young men had gotten tired of traveling and were given out, and they committed suicide together.

At noon we marched to the Yellowstone River and got up on a big hill, where we made camp. We were only a week behind Sitting Bull, but the two generals' commands waited there, because General Terry had sent for ten thousand more soldiers from Fort Leavenworth. Our soldiers had a great time fishing and hunting, while Sitting Bull must have crossed over into the British Possession by this point. Luck was with him, since the rivers were high and hard to cross. Well, there we sat, using up our rations, relieved when a boat finally arrived to resupply us.

Our most able scout, Buffalo Bill Cody, announced that he was going to go home on this boat, down to Omaha and then back by railroad to North Platte. He could see that there wasn't going to be any fight with Sitting Bull, that the soldiers were keeping just far enough away to avoid an encounter.

Finally General Crook's command recrossed the Powder River and marched down back to where we had come from. General Crook sent orders not to shoot, so that we wouldn't alert the Indians of our whereabouts, so we killed prairie chickens with clubs, which made handy food at the time. The next day we marched into the Little Missouri River valley, where we found a Sioux graveyard. The Indians put up four poles and spread some sticks and brush and blankets on it, then put a dead body up there under the sky. There must have been some treasures up there. One of the soldiers took some very large, fine blankets and several other things and took them to camp, but when the officers found out about it they made him take all those things back and fix the graves up as good as new.

We were now down on the Missouri River, and our scouts reported that they found the bodies of five men and three women who were killed by Sioux. They were naked and scalped, and we dug up a large hole and put them in and put earth on the decaying bodies. The scouts didn't find any fresh Indian tracks, though.

From everything I had heard of the Missouri River, I expected it to be a great, wide, deep, foaming stream. I was surprised to find just a little water flowing, and then dry spots for miles, and then a little water flowing again. For six days we traveled along the river, heading east toward Fort Lincoln, Dakota. We were running out of food, and we had to cut back rations to one hardtack biscuit a day, with just a little coffee and a little sugar. There was no more bacon, and General Crook said we still had another 125 miles to get to the fort. He changed his mind and decided to go up into the Black Hills. We saw plenty of buffalo, but we couldn't shoot them. We ran out of coffee and drank sugar water. Finally, after a march without eating, we came to a waterhole where some animals had died. The officers ordered the men to skin any dead horses, but there wasn't any meat on them. I found a tail and made some soup. Some of the men said that they had seen a fat dead horse back down the road about three miles away, and I told my friend Lieutenant Bishop that I was going to go with them to get some meat. There were probably Indian scouting parties back there, and Lieutenant Bishop said, "You better not forget your Henry rifle." I told him it was too heavy for me to carry it and meat at the same time, and he said, "Well, there lies my pistol. Take that, so that you can fight like a little man."

The soldiers had already gone off, and I caught up with them at a little gap in the hills. There was a man there, Sergeant Lynch, who told us to move quietly and not stand up straight, just creep along. He was an old fighting soldier who knew the Apaches. So the men went running off, watching and listening. The night was very dark, there being no moon, but we could plainly see the edges of the hills in the west. At last someone whispered that there was the horse, and we went to skin it. We got the meat and the liver and the tongue, then followed our tracks backward—although now someone was following us. We got back to camp, figuring that some Indians had also seen the horse. If they had got to the spot before us, they would have got the horsemeat and most likely our hides too.

We lived on horsemeat and berries, like Plains Indians, while General Crook sent Major Mills of the Third Cavalry off to Cooke City or Deadwood to get rations. He took about 350 men with him. The rest of the command moved ahead slowly, since many of the horses had died and so many soldiers were now on foot. Word came back from Major Mills that he was surrounded by several hundred Indians and needed help, so General Crook ordered the rest of the regiments to march as fast as they could. My horse was trailing, and some of the soldiers told me that I'd better kill him and eat some horsemeat, saying, "You can get over the country faster without that old horse." But I kept on driving my horse until I got up into the mountains to camp at a place called Milkwater Creek, where Lieutenant Bishop told me to turn my horse out with the rest of the herd. He gave me something to eat, a soup made of boiled buffalo jerky and wild onions, and it was good.

After resting for a while we moved on, going down the left side of a hill below which some Indians were making a fight. There were only three or five of them, but they were well dug in. Frank Grouard signaled us not to show ourselves, but Buffalo Chip stuck his head up and yelled, "Get up on your feet! Show me where the Indians are, and I will show you how I shoot them!" A shot rang out, and the boy was dead, shot in the forehead; thus ended the life of that boy of the plains, Buffalo Chip. Frank Grouard followed the smoke and found three Indian men in a dugout, and he killed them, and pretty soon there was no more shooting. This was about four in the afternoon.

We went through the Indian camp and gathered up buffalo meat and dried gooseberries, while the bugles sounded the order to stop fighting. Elsewhere some other Indians had fought with soldiers and driven away some of our horses. Frank Grouard went down to the ravine where the Indians were hiding out and asked what kind of Indians they were. They replied, Cheyenne. He was married to a Cheyenne in Indian Territory, so he could speak their language. General Crook told him to tell the Cheyenne to come out if they wanted to live; if they insisted on staying in the ravine, then he would break up their lodges and throw them down there and set the place on fire. When Frank Grouard said this, a chief came out, a tall man. He was shot through his stomach, and all he could do was to use both hands to hold the strings of his entrails as they hung out in front of him. There must have been twenty others in the hole with him. One was a woman who had been hit with bullets so often that she was mashed. Only sixteen of them were alive. They were told to stay in their tepees. The man who was shot through the stomach died before nightfall.

This band had been one of the straying parties of the Northern Cheyenne, with a few Arapahos. They had been with Sitting Bull until he crossed over the Yellowstone, when they separated from him and started going south. They said they had been about 1,500 in number. They said they had never killed any white men or fought with any soldiers, that Sitting Bull had killed many soldiers, not them. A whole regiment of infantry was placed over them as guards. Other soldiers rounded up about three hundred of their ponies.

The next morning we found that two more of them had died during the night, and the captives were told to do with them what they usually did with their dead. So they pulled down the lodges and threw them on top of the bodies, and then set fire to them.

The soldiers were ready to march. I had no horse, but Lieutenant Bishop told me to go out and get a pony—or even two ponies. I ran out and roped one, and then the bugles blew, and a soldier said, "You got one to ride anyhow," and then we went off with the prisoners to General Crook's camp. This fight was later called the Slim Buttes Fight, and the chief's name was Yellow Hand, of Roman Nose's band. This chief Yellow Hand was the one who was shot through the stomach, and before he expired he said that the Cheyenne had nothing to do with Sitting Bull's band and said they had written passes from the agent at Fort Robbins, Nebraska, to leave the reservation and go north to hunt buffalo and antelope for the coming winter. General Crook said that he was sorry that his soldiers came across these innocent Indians and took them to be the wrong sort of people, but nevertheless, he added, he was ordered to hunt out all Indians who were out in the wild country, and they had no business being out there considering the present situation, especially with what the Sioux had been doing to the soldiers and other people.

I got my pony and rode past the burning lodges and the burning bodies of those Cheyenne Indians, going down the creek, and rode past that place where Buffalo Chip got his last medicine, and a little way down I overtook some soldiers, but they were not in the outfit I was in. I whipped my pony on, while some soldiers yelled at me to go faster because the Cheyenne were on my tail. They laughed at me, but I didn't listen.

A little way on I caught up with G Company. When we crossed another creek and passed some hills, shots rang out, wounding some men and killing some horses. Major Upham ordered two or three companies to lay for the Indians who were shooting at them from across the valley. A, B, and G Troops dismounted. I was eager to have a chance to shoot at some Indians, so I dismounted my pony and left it with those who were holding the horses. Instead of staying with G Troop I went across a little gulch and joined up with the B Troop boys, who were lying on the ground and shooting across a little valley over into the hills. I took several shots with my Henry rifle.

While I was busy doing this, the soldiers mounted up and went off across the gulch before I knew it. I ran back to get my pony, but the soldiers had galloped off out of sight, and I could see only brush and rocks and prairie grass. I had enough sense to know that if I followed the soldiers I would be right in sight of the Indians, so I headed off under the cover of a ravine. Then I wound up on plain bottomland, and I looked back and saw several Indians on the hill across. I tried to run faster but couldn't. Some shots came at me, and one struck some stones and glanced up at my leg, and I dropped and thought I'd been hit but saw no blood. So I went on a little, and then I saw that some Indians were on the run across a creek below me to head me off at the top of the hill, about eight or ten of them. They were only two hundred yards away from me. I thought that day would be my last, and then I thought, well, I'll shoot every Indian I can until I get to the last of my cartridges.

I expected to be shot at any moment, but then I looked back and, to my surprise and relief, saw rows of horsemen shooting. Lieutenant Bishop yelled at me to move on up, saying, "Mike, are you alive? I thought I'd find you with your head off!" He had brought the whole company to get me, figuring that the Cheyenne would have tortured me when they found out I was another kind of Indian.

When I got to camp, Lieutenant Bishop was waiting for me, laughing about how I'd been left behind and nearly got killed. I said that I had wanted so bad to fight the Indians, and he said that no Indians had ever done me any harm, so that I shouldn't feel vengeful, and anyway I was small and young and had no business fighting anybody. Maybe the Indians had seen that I was just a small boy and wanted to catch me to get me out of the way, I thought, or maybe they wanted to torture me good.

I asked where my pony was, and Lieutenant Bishop said that a note had come from headquarters saying that all the ponies captured at the Slim Buttes Fight were to be slaughtered for issue as rations. I asked him to write me a note to get my pony back, and he wrote out a note and handed it to me, and I ran down to headquarters and found General Crook at home. He was very glad to see me, and he took both my hands in his and asked what the trouble was, so I handed him the note, and he read it, and then said, "It might be too late, my Apache boy. I am very sorry to take your only pony away from you, but I will do what I can to get it back to you, if possible." So he handed me another note and told me to run to the quartermaster general, who would secure my pony. I went to the quartermaster general, who told me to look through the ponies and find mine. I couldn't find him, and he told me that it must have been among the ponies that had already been killed, so there was nothing to be done about it now.

I almost cried when I heard that my pony had been killed. I would have to travel on foot for the rest of the campaign. The next morning we ate horsemeat for breakfast, and Lieutenant Bishop told me that I had to join the foot gang. Then he gave me a chunk of cooked horsemeat for lunch.

15

It had been raining all night, and the ground was very muddy. We went over limestone country, with cedar trees on the hills, and went down into a valley with a little creek in it that looked like milk. We used the water anyway.

The next morning, before daylight, I was told to join the foot gang, since we were going to have to make a long-distance march that day. I had a little piece of horsemeat left, and I made a little fire and cooked it and had a bite, then went to join the foot gang. Some of them had already gone on. There must have been eight hundred men in the gang whose horses had given out, or had been killed and eaten by the command. Some of the men asked me if I had any spare horsemeat, but I told them I had eaten the last of it for breakfast. I did not know if there would be any more meat to eat when we got to camp. We marched until evening time and then made camp again. When I met up with Lieutenant Bishop, he asked me what I had had to eat that day. I told him that I had only eaten a little piece of horsemeat. "Well," he said, "I've got a little bit of dried gooseberries left. That's the only thing I've had all day." I had dried gooseberries for supper.

I went back to the gang the next morning, and we were told to make at least forty miles that day across the muddy desert. From time to time some of the men would rush off, and after a while I went along to see what they were about. They were making for gopher holes, which were surrounded by wild onions. They would gather these and eat them. Sometimes we would find prickly pear, and then the men would set fire to them and burn off the thorns, then cut the pads up into chunks and eat them. I did the same in order to have something in my stomach and stay alive.

When we got to camp someone said that two soldiers had been scalped in sight of the whole command, but there were no soldiers able-bodied enough to go after the Indians. The Indians had been on the watch for stray soldiers ever since we left the Slim Buttes Fight. These two men had gotten permission to hunt deer or antelope, and the Indians were laying for them and shot them dead off their horses. And then they scalped them in plain sight.

The night was very dark, so that the boys ahead of us had had to whistle so we could follow them. We crossed the Belle Fourche River, which was not very large. I had no idea what direction we were marching in, and the sky was dark with clouds, and we were weak from hunger, almost crazed.

Many men strayed off and, tired of the soldier's way of life, committed suicide.

The next morning several men ran off up the creek, and I followed them, and we found trees full of wild plums. The creek bottom was full of them. We shook the trees and picked up the plums and ate until I was sick.

The command stayed there that day, and the sun shone brightly for the first time in nearly two weeks. Someone said we were near the Black Hills, up on the north end, and that in a few hours wagons would come full of rations for the whole command, with plenty of beef. I was anxious to see those wagons coming when I heard about the beef. I couldn't have gone on another mile. Finally someone saw a wagon down on the road, and then another, and then herds of animals. All day long we watched the wagons rolling, passing us by to get to the rest of the command, and finally coming to our camp, too. That afternoon 175 head of cattle were killed and 150 wagons full of all kind of grub were distributed through the quartermaster general, who gave us double rations. The men brought loads down on their backs: flour, bread, coffee, sugar, beef, bacon. When night came we were eating, and the next day we were ordered to remain in camp and eat all we could, and to shoot our guns in rejoicing and thanks for living, and then to clean our guns the following day.

I ate so much that I got diarrhea. The whole command had dysentery, and the doctors had to go from camp to camp to give medicine to the men. I thought I was going to die, until the doctors gave me some medicine and told me I would be all right in two or three days. Lieutenant Bishop had it worse than me. He couldn't even get up on his feet. I was well and could eat a square meal after a while, but we had to stay there in camp for six days.

The whole command moved on toward the Black Hills and came to a little town called Cooke City, where many of the men got drunk and started to fight. General Crook had intended to stay there for two or three days, but the men would not be good, so he ordered a march on to Deadwood. He changed his mind about going into town, figuring that the men would behave the same, and stopped about fifteen miles away from Deadwood and sent a few men in to get supplies. They came back with wagons loaded with grub, enough for about a week, sufficient to get us to the Red Cloud Agency.

We kept on marching, camping in the thick pine trees. We burned nothing but pine wood, and because the nights were getting pretty cool we stood close to the fire, and we all got dark from the smoke of the pitchy wood. There was a Jewish boy in G Troop who had a dark complexion, and he was shining black on that march; you couldn't tell him from a Negro.

We must have marched the whole length of the Black Hills, and we were in the thick pine woods for at least twelve days. On some fine sunny days the men and even the officers would take off their clothes and shake them over the fire, laughing and saying, "This way I'll kill some of the bugs that have been biting me all night and keeping me from sleep." I thought I was the only lousy one until then. We had had no change of clothing for three months, marching all the time. We had put on our clothing at the headwaters of the Tongue River in late August. Now it was going on November.

The next day we marched down a canyon and came to a creek and camped there. The cook had made dried peaches for supper. Again I ate so much that I was sick all night, and I was so weak the next day that I couldn't walk. So Lieutenant Bishop asked Captain Hayes, who was in charge of the company, to lend me a horse. Captain Hayes said that I could ride to the Red Cloud Agency, and I could have the horse for as long as I needed.

On that day the whole command divided into columns to come into the agency from all directions. The foot gang was to march straight there. General Crook was ordered to do this so that he could cut off any stray bands going north to join Sitting Bull, whom General Howard had followed up to the British Possession. That was as far as the soldiers could go, even in wartime.

At about two or three in the afternoon the command came together at the Red Cloud Agency, where the great chief Red Cloud lived. He and his band of Sioux had decided to be peaceable with the soldiers and other white people. He made no kick against the whites going into the Black Hills. That evening he held a meeting with General Crook. Frank Grouard was there, and he interpreted for Red Cloud, even though he was a white man and Red Cloud was a Sioux chief. Grouard was married to a Cheyenne woman down in Fort Reno, in the Indian Territory. The Cheyenne used to go to war alongside the Sioux, so they could understand one another's language. I was not present when the meeting was held, nor did I ever hear about the results of the consultation between General Crook and Red Cloud.

The man who had loaned me a horse the day before was named Jack McGilligan. He was the very man who had dragged me off the rock where I was sitting on December 22, 1872, a little north of the Four Peaks. He was always kind to me and often gave me presents, and he had not hesitated to give me a horse.

That morning, after all the companies were called together, they were told that they would be going to different posts. Some would go to Fort Laramie, Wyoming, the headquarters of the Fifth Cavalry, and others to Fort Russell, Wyoming, about three miles north of Cheyenne. Six or seven companies were going to go to Fort Sidney, Nebraska, and some of them would go farther, to Fort McPherson. I presume that this ended the campaign of 1876 against Sitting Bull.

The commands were given wagons. Fort Sidney was said to be 150 miles from the Red Cloud Agency, so I was told to get into our wagon for the journey. It took us about six days to get to Fort Sidney. The country around was bare of trees and bushes, and when we got there it was freezing. Some soldiers got drunk that night, and the next morning it was reported that two men from M Troop had lain out all night and froze to death. The little command turned out and buried them in the best military style, and in the afternoon Major Lieb marched M Troop and some others—I think C and G—out of that bad place and, in the next three days, took them to Fort McPherson. We followed the Platte River all the way down. We passed a town called North Platte, but the command did not stop to camp there for fear that the soldiers would get drunk, with the same results as at Fort Sidney.

Major Lieb and Lieutenant Keyes were court-martialed and dismissed from the army. They were ordered to Fort Brown, Wyoming, at the Shoshone Agency, in September 1877. The next year some Arapahos and Cheyenne came from Fort Sheridan, Nebraska. The Shoshone chief was Washakie, and many who saw him said that he was the very image of the great George Washington. He was big and tall, a fine-looking man, with long white hair thrown back over his forehead, and he always rode a white horse. He had three sons: the oldest was big and fat, but the other two were middle-sized young men. A medicine man came with them, wearing all kinds of feathers in a great war bonnet. I watched him perform the peace pipe ceremony, holding the pipe in the air, and bringing it to the ground, and then smoking for a little bit before passing it to the man sitting farthest away, who would do the same as the medicine man did, and then pass it to another man. The chief got the pipe last.

The officers would come out of their houses and watch the Indians, who were seated on the ground in a circle. An interpreter called Friday came with them. He had been with the army for twenty-five years, named so because he had been captured on a Friday. He spoke very good English but could not read or write.

On the way to Fort Brown we stopped at the Green River Station, on the Union Pacific Railroad. I was strolling along a little creek when I saw some bright yellow things in the water, and I took some of them and brought them to camp and showed them to Lieutenant Bishop. He only said, "Keep it. It will come in good some day." So I wrapped them in a piece of white cloth and put them in my pocketbook. Two years later, in Cheyenne, I took them to a jewelry shop, and the man there weighed them and said they were worth $4.75. I told him, "Give it to me," and he did. I didn't know it was so valuable; I just thought it was shiny dust. But I was told later that it was pure gold. I often wish that I could go back to that little stream.

Fort Brown, three miles from the Shoshone Indian Agency, is, I think, the highest in altitude of any military post in the Union. It sits right on the east side of the Rocky Mountains, by Fremont Peak, one of the highest in America. There is a nice little valley there and a stream of water that flows down into the Wind River, which is the headwater of the great Colorado River of Arizona. Just below the post, about a mile and a half away, is a hot spring, and on the north side of the creek is a tar spring where the soldiers got tar for the roofs and sidewalks at the post.

I think I ruined my health at the hot springs. I had borrowed a horse from somebody on the post to ride out into the valley. I came to the hot spring, and it looked too good to pass, so I tied the horse to a bush and got into the water up to my neck. Then I heard a horse running, and I looked to where I had tied my horse, and he wasn't there. I got out with my shoes in my hands and ran down the road toward the post. I was afraid that the horse would stray and go off to some other country, with a new saddle and bridle. I ran back to the post so fast that my feet hardly touched the ground. It was snowing and the wind was blowing fiercely, blowing right into my face. I tried to get out of the wind, and walked a little, and then ran some more, and finally got back to the post. The horse had reached home all right, and he would have got home at any rate without my running after him all that distance like a fool.

A few days later, I took to bed sick, and the pain and illness settled all through me. I was coughing, and the doctor said that I would not live long. Lieutenant Bishop doctored me with some lemon and brandy and hot water all mixed up, and fed me, and in a few days I was well enough to eat and drink anything I wanted.

Before that happened I could beat anybody running a foot race at any distance—75 yards, 100 yards, 250 yards, half a mile, three miles. I used to keep up with horses running five or seven miles, running alongside them. There was a small town close to the post called Lander, about thirteen miles away, and parties of soldiers would go there on horse. I would be on foot, and the soldiers would trot fast to try to tire the little Apache boy out. I would always get to Lander before them, and then beat them back to the post too. Their horses would be tired out, and the men were mad, but I was just as fresh as before.

One time this old prospector wanted to run a footrace, and the boys in G Troop got up a purse of $150 for a hundred-yard dash. I beat the man by about fifteen yards, and then he wanted to go double or nothing for two hundred yards. I said no, thinking it was too far for me to make good time. But the boys said, "Oh, hell, run anyhow, you can beat the old man at any distance." So I went on and ran the race, but I stepped on a sharp stone and came near falling, and when

I straightened out he passed the line about five yards ahead of me. I have never done any foot racing since.

In the spring of 1878 about 750 Northern Cheyenne and Arapahos came from, I think, Fort Sheridan to the Shoshone Agency. They were told to make their homes down the creek, about five miles away, near the hot spring. I used to go down there with the boys my age, and sometimes I would stay with them for two or three days at a time. I could understand the Arapaho language, and I could use sign language, too. Most all of the Plains Indians used sign language, but I never knew the Apaches or any other tribe in the Southwest to do so. The Lipan and Mescalero Apaches in New Mexico used sign language, but they traveled out on the plains. I played with the young boys, and when I could not understand their words they would make signs, moving their hands just like they were talking.

There came news that a band of Bannock Indians from Fort Hall, Idaho, were on the warpath, and were making toward Yellowstone National Park. Orders came to enlist seventy-five scouts from the Northern Cheyenne and Arapahos, and fifty more from the Shoshone. Nobody knew that the Shoshone were related to the Bannock. Lieutenant Bishop was told to take fifty of the best, most able-bodied men and these scouts and go cut off the Indians. I went with my old friend, just as I did on whatever peril he undertook to do.

On the first night out we camped on the Wind River, following it to Yellowstone for two days. When we came to the head of the river, Lieutenant Bishop ordered the scouts to search for the Bannocks. Some of the Cheyenne and Arapaho scouts weren't sure what to do if they came across any hostile Indians, but Lieutenant Bishop told them to fight them if they showed up to fight, and to shoot them on sight. The Shoshone did not much care to go out with the scouting parties. They hunted for deer or cattle to eat. I went out with the hunting party, going out the way we came in, toward the valley of the Wind River.

A man by the name of Sergeant Steele brought us a yearling steer, and a fat one, too. Back in camp the next day, some scouts came in dressed up for war, with scalps on sticks and drums made of head skin. They had been attacking the hostile Indians when some of the Shoshone came along and saved their kinfolk, so that seven men escaped. The other three men in the party were killed, and thirteen women and children were taken prisoner. That night the Cheyenne and Arapaho were having a great time singing about their victory, but the headmen among the Shoshone went to Lieutenant Bishop and asked him to make the Cheyenne and Arapaho stop singing and dancing over what they had killed, since they were part of the same people. The Shoshone said that they would fight them in camp if they didn't stop. Lieutenant Bishop was a man who was never afraid of anything, but he thought it best to quiet things down, so he went to the Cheyenne and Arapaho leaders and explained the facts.

Yellowstone was only about fifteen miles away from where we were. Through Shoshone interpreters the captured women said that only a few Bannocks had left the reservation and were going to visit their Shoshone relatives. Most of the others had already gone back home. If they were on the warpath, they said, would they have come this way? They could not hope to fight against the soldiers in such small numbers.

The next day Lieutenant Bishop ordered his little command to return to post. It took three days to get back, and the Cheyenne and Arapaho scouts went back home and told about their victory. Their women wanted to make a celebration, but they were warned not to do so lest the Shoshone attack.

The captured Bannocks may have been making excuses, as everybody does when caught doing something bad. Whether they told the truth or not, nevertheless those Indians had not done any killing, nor had they stolen any animals, so you could not say they were bad Indians. The captured Bannocks were returned to Fort Hall, and that was the end of the scare. It turned out that the authorities at Fort Hall had wanted the Bannocks to move to some other place, but they did not like where they were going and protested. The agent insisted with much ferocity that he could have the soldiers make them move anywhere he wanted whenever he wanted. The Indians were satisfied where they were, but when they heard this they started off for the hills where they used to live, not molesting anyone or stealing anything. After all this the agent at Fort Hall was fired.

In the fall of 1878 I witnessed the Cheyenne and Arapahos dancing a Sun Dance. They set up a large pole, in the middle of which they fastened a buffalo's head. Six men were seated around it, beating on a large bass drum. The dancers were naked and painted and had little whistles that they kept in their mouths. Every man had to dance for thirty days, and anyone who stopped had to give up some horses. When they danced they were supposed to look at the buffalo's head, and when they got to the foot of the pole they raised their hands toward heaven, then started backward, still looking at the buffalo's head. They did this for nearly a week without any drinking water or food, which is positively prohibited. The Indians did this kind of dancing in order to keep up their great endurance during times of war. If they were chased by enemies they could outlast them, riding for a long time without thirst or hunger. The young men were strictly trained, and I have known some of them drop from dancing, too weak to move. The glare of the sun above them was the Great Spirit, for the Indian race has a universal belief that the sun is their father, just as the whites have a belief in there being a God and the Savior. Some of the young men were foolish enough to heed their elders' advice to be tied to a post with a rope that went through their breasts. They would go back and forth along the rope, and sometimes the flesh would break, which would make the young man a great warrior, because he never feared the great pains upon him.

I was there when Fort Brown was changed to Fort Washakie in honor of the great Shoshone chief. I have seen winters there where it got so cold that the Wind River was frozen so solid that wagons could cross it for four or five months.

There is a place called Bull Lake right in the Rockies, about fifteen miles from the fort, where you can get fine large trout. I have never seen more of them in any other lake or stream. I was out there once with a party of soldiers. There was no wagon road within a dozen miles at the time, so there was just a horse road. We took wagons as far as we could and then rode in and fished for about five days. The largest trout was nine pounds, and the rest were four or five or seven pounds. At any rate, we got tired of eating fish all the time, and we went back to the post.

In the fall of 1878, Lieutenant Bishop was promoted to first lieutenant and had to join Company A, Fifth Cavalry, with Captain Jacob Auger in command. The company was at Fort D. A. Russell. In the late part of October Lieutenant Bishop told me to get ready to leave, and we took the stage to Green River, and there we got on the train to Cheyenne and then proceeded to the fort. We were only there for about a month when six companies were posted out toward the White River Agency. This was where the Utes had killed Agent Meeker and captured the agent's little girl. Major Thornburgh was ordered out from Fort Collins, but the Utes were on the lookout and saw him coming. Chief Ouray's whole band went out and waited for Major Thornburgh near the rim of the mountain, at a narrow divide. They shot the commander down first, and some other men too, and the ones who were still alive got into a deep gulch and hid. They could not raise their heads to shoot, and there was no water for the men or animals. A few men got out of their hiding places under darkness of night and made their way to the railroad station on foot, and that way the news got out all over the country in short order, and soldiers came in from all over. Lieutenant Bishop did not want me to go with him that time, because he had house furniture and a new buggy that he wanted me to take care of. I didn't care much about going anywhere so late in the year, because it was good and freezing by then, and still only November. Before he left me he made some arrangements for me to be boarded with a detachment that was left behind. He gave me a twelve-dollar monthly allowance at the sutler's store, not to exceed it.

The Fifth Cavalry went down to White River, where Chief Ouray gave himself up. The Meeker girl was freed, and the Utes went back to the White River Agency. After about two months, the soldiers returned to Fort Russell.

In the spring of 1879, the Fifth Cavalry under General Merritt moved its headquarters to Fort Laramie. When we moved there, Lieutenant Bishop urged me to go to day school with the soldiers' children. I brought my books home, and Lieutenant Bishop helped me with my lessons in the evenings. I only went for about four months and went ahead of all the rest of the class I was put in. I studied by myself after that and got into the second grade.

In the next year, 1880, in the summertime, I was asked to ride the mail route between the fort and Sidney Bridge, a distance of about a hundred miles. The contractor said that I had to have four horses, one to change off every twenty-five miles. Some of the other men usually made the trip in three days for fifteen dollars a job. I told the man I would do it, and he said, you can do it in two days and get your money quicker. I started off early one morning at a run and got to the first station about twenty-five miles away. Then I went to the second

station, thirty-five miles from there, and got there at noon, and then
the next station about twenty-five miles away at about two o'clock,
and then the last station thirty-five miles on before sundown. I got
a little food and two bottles of beer and had a pretty good dinner,
and then had the horses saddled up in short order, and then I started
off homeward about two hours later. I didn't have to deliver the mail
going home, so I just changed horses. The night was dark and threatening to rain, and the only way I could see the road was by lightning
flashes. I rode on past the last station and went a few miles, but then
I couldn't see the road. I tied my horse to a tree and slept for a while
under my overcoat.

I have often heard that ghosts go after people at night. I have
found that ghost stories are meant to scare people. I traveled across
the Laramie River bottom for many miles in dark night, a place full
of the skeletons of whites and Indians, and I could see small pieces of
bone and ruined villages when I rode. I went over all these human
bones, but I heard nothing from them all those nights of traveling.
There was even a place where soldiers had slaughtered some Indians
who made no attempt to fight back. It is foolish to believe that parts
of dead persons can come back to life enough to harm anyone. So I
would advise.

I made only three trips along the mail route until General Merritt
told Lieutenant Bishop to ask me if I wanted to go to school regularly,
since there was nothing to learn from being around the soldiers all
the time. Without considering the matter much, I said yes, since I
was always willing to do anything that would better me. Lieutenant
Bishop said that the general had handed him a letter and told him to
go to the quartermaster and get things in readiness for a long journey.

In September 1880 Lieutenant Bishop took me on the government
stage to Cheyenne and saw me off on the train. We held hands, and
he shed tears and I did too, thinking about all the times he had helped
me and cared for me when I was sick. He loved me as a child, and I
respected him as a father, but that day we were going to part, and
there was no telling whether we would ever meet again. He only said
that he would telegraph our old friend Captain E. D. Thomas to meet
me at Omaha.

Captain Thomas met me there and drove me out in an ambulance
to Fort Omaha, about four miles away. In the evening he took me to

see General and Mrs. Crook. She remembered me well, even though I had not seen her since 1873 at Fort Whipple, when I went with Mrs. Burns's children to her house. They both greeted me warmly and wished me great success in my new undertaking. Mrs. Crook said to me, "Mike, schooling is a great thing. That is the way the white men got the best of the Indians. Now you are an Indian, and an Apache too, that tribe that the white people consider to be very bad. They do not want the Apaches to have the chance to be worth something, but you will do your best to get a thorough education, and be useful to your people, and make the white people change their minds. The good Indians are those who are dead, but the living are better ones yet."

The next morning, after breakfast, Captain Thomas took me to the depot at Omaha City, and when he put me on the train he gave me a bill, which I discovered was a twenty-dollar greenback, and told me to make it last as long as I could. He got off as the train was getting ready to pull away, and he shed tears, and I did too. He was the officer who was with Captain James Burns in December 1872 at the Four Peaks, and who called me Mickie, while James Burns gave me his name, making me Michael Burns.

16

I arrived at the Carlisle School in late September 1880. Captain Richard H. Pratt was the superintendent, and Dr. Given the assistant superintendent. Dr. Given was well known by the Kiowas and Comanches and Lipan Apaches near Fort Sill. Miss Robinson was the field matron, and Mr. Campbell the school disciplinary. There were about 175 students from all kinds of Indian tribes, but I was the one from farthest west, as an Apache Indian from Arizona. I had already been to third grade, but there was hardly anyone else in the school who had got that far, so I had to study by myself. We had school in the forenoon, and in the afternoon I was put to work. I went to carpentry, then blacksmithing, then back to carpentry, and on other days would be put to farming. On Saturdays all the boys would police the whole grounds, and on Sundays we went to Sunday school in the morning, and in the afternoon Dr. Lippincott preached. He was a nice talker, and I never heard anyone preach about God's teaching through his son Jesus Christ as well as he did. I sometimes went to town to hear others preach, but they did not preach with such good feelings. When we had spare time I taught the other boys how to play baseball, which I had learned from the soldiers in Wyoming. I had a pretty hard time trying to make the boys play baseball, but the next year we formed a team.

In the summer of 1881 I was sent to a farm in New York State, in Orange County, close to the Hudson River, about nine miles south of Newburgh and about seven miles west of the military academy at West Point. The owner was a man named Mr. Valentine of New York City. He was the inventor of a method of varnishing and owned two or three large stores there. The farm grew mostly apples, but we also milked 175 cows every night. There were eight other boys there, but only one of them was Indian, a Creek named Almarine McKellip. There was also a Pueblo Indian girl, Mary, from the Rio Grande

Mike Burns while enrolled as a student at the Carlisle Indian School, Pennsylvania.

above Albuquerque. We boys would hoe the corn or pick apples, then start milking at about three o'clock, and then load the milk onto railroad cars on the side tracks to take to the city.

When the winter came on, the Indian boy and girl went back to Carlisle, but I was told to stay and go to the country school. I agreed to do so. I was getting $18.00 a month and board, and I was promised that I could go to school about two miles off. I worked at night and before breakfast and after school for my board and wages. I milked those 175 cows and did other work, and I went to school, too.

When spring came, I wrote to General Wesley Merritt, who was in command at West Point, and he wrote me back and asked me to come and see him. I asked the farm foreman, Major Alvoh, if I could get off and showed him General Merritt's letter. He had been in the war and didn't like the general, but it didn't take him long to approve. The next morning I walked to the train station, about three miles away, and went to Newburgh, where there was a boat belonging to the Military Academy. I told the captain that I was going to see my old friend General Merritt. He said, "Well, you know the general! For how long?" I told him that I was on the campaign against the Sioux in 1876, after Sitting Bull killed Custer and his men. I hadn't seen the general for a long time, and it would be a bad policy for a man not to meet his old friends when he had the chance to do so. "Well," he said, "I am an old friend of the general's, too," and told me to get in. He asked me whether I had killed any Sioux. I told him that I wasn't sure, but I had shot my gun a lot of times, and I was quite sure that I couldn't have helped hitting someone. I told him about General Crook and General Merritt, and about having had to eat horsemeat for a whole month. When he heard that the captain shook his head and said, "Eat horsemeat? I couldn't even think about eating horses."

Some men sitting close by heard what I had said. One of them said, "It's true about them eating horsemeat. I read a book about that war against the Sioux Indians, and General Crook's command was out of food for several weeks and had to eat their horses to stay alive." He said, "Well, it must have been hard times that you seen, but you look mighty young to be out at war." I answered that I may have looked young, but I had still been out on the Starvation Campaign. "Well, sir," he said, "you have a great history behind you. Now get a good education and use it so that you can write a nice little history about yourself and what you have seen. Now we're at our landing, and if I had the time I would take you to General Merritt myself, but I have to get to the city by seven, and here it is noon." So he bade me farewell, asking me to give the general his name, but that was so long ago that I have forgotten it.

I was shown the way to General Merritt's quarters. A man went with me and called at the door, and a colored mistress appeared, and the young officer told her to tell the general that a young stranger wanted to see him. The young colored lady went back, and there appeared the great big man, who recognized me at once and called me by my name. "Why, there is Mike, an Apache boy of the Fifth Cavalry!" he said. I said, "General, I am happy to see you, sir." The general turned around and said to the officer, "Here is an Apache boy of Arizona who was in the Fifth Cavalry, my regiment. Captain Burns and Lieutenant Thomas captured him in 1872. Please shake hands with him."

A few minutes later Mrs. Merritt came, and we all dined. Afterward the general took me to the hotel and secured a room for me, then took me back to his house, where we spent much time talking about fighting Indians and crossing the Badlands and the Starvation Campaign. He asked me whether I had been affected by diarrhea, and I told him I thought I was the only one who suffered from it, but he said that the whole command had had it, keeping the doctors on the run dispensing medicine. At four o'clock he had his fine black carriage brought to the house. The driver was a black man dressed in a white suit and black shiny hat. General and Mrs. Merritt and myself got in, and we drove around the grounds where the cadets were parading. The cadets all saluted the carriage, and me in it too.

After it was over the general took me back to the hotel, and I slept through the night, a good sleep. The next morning the carriage was at the front of the hotel, with the same driver, who told me that the general wanted me to come to his house. I got in the carriage and sat where the general sat. The general was at his door, ready to receive me. He took me over to the parade ground where the cadets drilled, and then he asked me, "How would you like to be one of those cadets you've seen drilling and dressed in all kinds of uniforms? In about five years' time you'll be an officer in the army, and then be sent out to join any regiment that has a vacancy." He told me to think about it.

But being a young man who had no sense, I foolishly said no. I had too much work to do back at the farm, and I couldn't have done both jobs. The general said nothing more, but asked when I wanted to go home. In the morning, I said, if there was a boat to Newburgh. He told me that one went at 7:30 in the morning and another at 2:30 in the afternoon. I said I wanted to go on the first one.

This was in the year 1881, close on to winter. I could have been a cadet, and in five years I could have been a second lieutenant in any army regiment. I could have joined the cavalry, or the infantry, or the artillery, or been sent out to Arizona to join the Geronimo War with the Sixth or Seventh Cavalry in 1886. I could have been drawing a salary of $125.00 a month, instead of being a scout, where I was drawing only $25.00—but then I was out of a job and had to go out and cut wood for $6.00 a cord. I might have been in the army for the last thirty years. I might have been killed in some war. I might have become a high-ranking officer. I might have lived too high and gotten sick and died that way. As it is, on the whole, I am glad that I went back to the simple life and have worked hard to earn a living.

The next day I went back to the Valentine farm and stayed there until the spring of 1882, when I made up my mind to go back to Carlisle School. First I wanted to take in the scenery on the Hudson River. I went by boat to Jersey City, about fifty-six miles. The captain of the boat, the man I had met before, invited me up to the top of the boat and pointed out all of the places of interest, such as where the British soldiers fought the Americans at the time of the Revolutionary War. We got to Jersey City near evening, and I changed boats and crossed the river to New York City, the big place I had heard so much about and which I wanted to see, but it was raining so hard that I went only a few blocks and stopped and found a hotel. I did have the chance to see the great Brooklyn Bridge, which was only about half finished, with great ships passing under it going up the East River. It was raining hard, but there were still lots of men working on the bridge. Then I went back to Jersey City and took a train for Philadelphia, as I wanted to see it too. When I got there, it was still raining and was very foggy, so I only stayed one night and the next morning went to Harrisburg, and then to Carlisle.

Captain Pratt had gathered about fifty new pupils from the Cheyenne and Arapahos at the Darlington Agency near Fort Reno, in the Indian Territory, and another seventy-five Sioux from the Standing Rock, Sisseton, Yankton, and Oglala agencies. There was one young fellow among the Cheyenne with long hair who was as white as could be. He was called White Buffalo, and he was a fast runner, too.

As before, the pupils went to school half a day and then worked the other half. The boys and girls came together in the classroom, but at mealtimes the boys were called together in lines and rows just like soldiers. One of the boys was the first sergeant. Mr. Campbell would call off our names and we had to answer immediately or get marked absent, and then we would have to miss a meal or even get sent to the guardhouse.

Carlisle Barracks had been built by the old soldiers called the Hessians in the Revolution, I think around 1778. Most people said it was used as a recruiting station for the Union Army during the Civil War, but afterward it was put to much better use for the Indians to be trained in the environments of civilization and education, so that the Indian race could be saved. Carlisle has turned out scholars and has placed many young Indian men and women in responsible positions, as many as any white men and women, so that the officers of the school can well be proud and say that their work has been well done.

I can't say, however, that I got a thorough normal education at Carlisle Indian School, because I didn't stay there long enough. I did not think I was getting on fast enough, as we had only half a day's school every day, and no one can progress very fast at that rate of study. I made up my mind to go someplace where I could go to school all day, and then work on Saturday for wages or board.

So in May 1882, Captain Pratt called me to his office and asked me if I wanted to go out into the country to work during the summer and then go to school in the winter. I was glad to accept the offer. He told me that Miss Robertson, the chief clerk, would escort me to Lore City, Ohio. The next morning Miss Robertson and I were on the train to Harrisburg, and then westbound to Pittsburgh, smoky and misty, where the sun could not be seen. We got a train going down the Ohio River to Wheeling, West Virginia, and then a westbound into Ohio, and finally we arrived at Lore City, where a man and his wife by the name of Johnson met us at the station. Mr. Johnson drove us to their home. I was expecting to see some great buildings, since it was called a city, but Lore City was very small, just three or four houses and the station.

Everyone around there was a Christian, belonging to the Presbyterian Church. Alvah Johnson had just lately married Lizzie Sprout. Mr. Sprout was the head of the church elders, and Mr. William Johnson, Alvah's father, was a trustee, as was Mr. McCullough, a farmer nearby. They showed me my work on the farm. I had to feed the milk cattle, and then at harvest I drove the hay wagon, and I husked the corn, and then I had to milk the cows and take the milk to the train station. I had to plow the fields in season, too. But in midwinter I stopped my farm work and went to school, which was about four miles away. I walked there with Alvah Johnson's sister, who was about fourteen, and Lizzie Johnson's sister Mary Sprout, and the three McCullough children. Some days when it snowed Alvah would take me and his sister Lillie to school.

I went to Christian meetings and listened to the teachings preached by good Christian workers. I was surrounded by neighbors, all good Christian people. So I got an education and learned Christianity, and was advised by those good Christian people how to learn the gospels so that I could go out west to my people as a missionary, to teach them about the Bible. The Apaches had never had anybody among them to tell them about God and his loving message so that they would stop fighting and become good people.

I stayed with these good people for two years. I went to school for two winters. I received a fair education and obtained some sensible English. I learned more than if I had stayed five years at Carlisle. But Alvah Johnson never said a word about what he owed me for working for him.

So I wrote a letter to Captain Pratt at Carlisle, saying that my scholarship had about expired and that I was thinking about going westward and saving some money to continue my schooling in the winter. I asked him to take my name from the rolls at Carlisle so that I could be free to go and work wherever I wanted to. Not long after that came an official letter addressed to Alvah Johnson. He read the letter to me and said, "Well, what do you think about this? Your old friend Captain Pratt says that you are no longer enrolled at Carlisle Indian School and that you can do as you wish now. I am going to make you a proposition. You have been living with me going on two years now, and I can say that you have done most satisfactory work, and the other neighbors speak very highly of you. If you choose to stay with me another year, there is a house and a barn and about twenty-five acres on a lot that you can have to start on. There are two nice-looking girls whom you have gone with to meetings and fairs, and I know that they would offer their whole souls to you as a husband. They are from the best families. There are plenty of young white men from the best families, too, but they care not a bit for them. We often hear from their parents that they would rather choose that young Indian lad than to have their daughters go with the white boys. This, I think, is in your best interest for the future. It is the best for you."

But even though I have not forgotten about Lulla and Annie, those two girls, I had made up my mind to go back west to Arizona, the land of my mother and father. So again I foolishly said no. Alvah Johnson looked sadly into Lizzie's face and said to her, "We have to lose Mike, I guess, since I cannot make him change his mind and he insists on going back west to his wild forest and desert."

So that August, Alvah Johnson bought a trunk for me, and I got ready. He still never said anything about how much he owed me for two years' work. I had saved about $85.00 before coming to Lore City. I was going out west as far as the money would last, and then I would have to work to go any farther.

One morning Mr. and Mrs. Johnson and all of the neighbors went with me to the train. The two girls were there. We got to the depot, and then Alvah Johnson went into the ticket office, came out, and handed me a ticket. Then he took a large roll of greenbacks from his pocket and counted it out in my hands: fives, tens, and twenties. He said, "Here is $275.00, and I bought a ticket for you to Atchison, Kansas. Is that the place I understand you wanted to go to?" All the time the two girls were holding my hands, standing right by my side. I got one of them free and put the money in my pocket. I gave each one of the girls $5.00, but they refused to accept the money, and one of them said, "You may need that money on your travels, so keep it." And I said all right, and then thanked them all. One of the girls sobbed bitterly, and I felt like doing so myself, and when the train rolled up I said, "I bid all of my friends good-bye, all of you good people. You have treated me with all kindness all the time I have been among you. You all knew that I am of a different race, not a white man but an Indian. Still I am not ashamed to say that I am an Indian. I am more proud than ever to be an Indian." Most of the womenfolk were sobbing by now.

The train pulled off, and I was soon out of sight of Lore City, Ohio. This was in August 1884.

A day later I arrived at Chicago, where I immediately boarded a train for Atchison. I took a train that was going up the Missouri River as far as Rulo, Nebraska. There I had a very good friend, El-wood Doran, an Iowa Indian I had met at Carlisle Indian School. He lived at the Sac and Fox Agency, and I had kept in touch with him. He had written letters to me in Lore City saying that I should come out and go hunting with him, because there was a lot of game nearby. He had sent me directions, and so I sent him a telegram saying I was coming. He met me at the depot when I pulled in around 11:00 a.m.

There were some other Indians with him, women and children, along with a man named Charles Kihiga, who was the son of an Iowa chief. (The Iowas live with the Sac and Fox.)

On our way to the Sac and Fox Agency, which was half in Kansas and half in Nebraska, they started acting funny. We were out on the road crossing the Big Nemaha River when I heard someone calling to the driver ahead to stop. Our four wagons pulled together and went off into the thick brush. We all got out. They took a large keg of beer out of the wagon, and some cups and a bucket, and everybody drank—men, women, and children. The barrel was emptied in a short time, and everyone was very drunk. The way they obtained the liquor was from whites and half-breeds, who could get whiskey as easily as any white man. The Indians pitched in a few dollars and got drunk. Beer was the favorite among the Sac and Fox Indians.

We got moving and arrived at my friend's home about midnight. The next morning Elwood took me over to the agency to make the acquaintance of the employees there, and they told Elwood that some of the buildings were badly in need of repair. The agent asked us if we would undertake the job. The government wage was $2.50 a day and board, the agent said, and he asked me if that was satisfactory. I said that it was all right by me, so the next morning we started in to work on the building. The roof was full of holes, and the windows were all broken, and there were no doors, and there was hardly a floor. All of it had to be fixed. We used to work together carpentering and painting at Carlisle, so it was not new work to us. We put the school into good shape, and then we painted it. We were at the job a little over a month, though some days we didn't work on account of bad weather. At any rate, I think we received somewhere around $75.00 each for the work.

Ministers came over to the agency from Highland, Kansas, to preach at times, and one of them told me that there was a fine school at Highland called Highland University, and if I wanted to go to it, there was a good chance I could get in, since I was young and of good moral character. I told this young Christian man that I had not got all the money I needed yet, but that I had earned $75.00, and if he wanted to take me to the school I would try to get in. He said he would be glad to do so, and he escorted me to the president, Professor McCarty. When I was paid about two weeks later I went to school and paid the tuition. This was in October 1884. The tuition fee was $12.50 a month, and board was $20.00 a month, and I had to pay for fuel and buy books, and every time I finished a grade I had to buy another set of books. It cost me $40.00 a month to stay at this school without spending any money foolishly, since I was attending a highly respected Christian school and I was a young Christian man. I had nearly $300.00 when I enrolled.

Professor McCarty asked me what kind of study I wanted to undertake, and I told him that I wanted to be a schoolteacher. He told me to take the normal course and showed me a class to join. In three months I went to a higher grade, and in two more months I went up to another, and Professor McCarty used to stand me up in front of the students and talk about how fast I was proceeding with my studies, while they came from educated families and could speak English well but were all very poor scholars now. "Mike Burns is an Apache Indian," he said, "and his parents could never speak the English language at all. They never saw a white man. A few years ago he couldn't even speak the English language. But give him the chance to improve his faculties, and he is far superior to you. He has been here only a few months and has surpassed all of you in your studies. He can go into the Academic Department next year if he chooses, but he only wanted to be able to teach school, and I am willing to give him his diploma at the end of this term so that he can go out to teach in any school in the state of Kansas."

This was in March 1885. I had paid all my bills in advance, because that was the rule. I stayed through April, but I could not raise enough to meet the monthly amount. The good Christian men and women often told me that if you listen to us good Christian people we will help you with anything you want. Before I was also studying to be a lawyer, but those Christian good talkers promised many things that they would do for me if I gave up that study, saying that it was not honorable, that no lawyer makes an honest living, because they always steal people's money and scheme to deprive people as much as stealing things outright. That is not honest, they said. You must change your course of study to Christianity, and we will help you get all the things you need for your education, and when you get your degree we will send you out west to your people, especially the Apaches, who are always at war with other people. You can teach them how to live right and throw away their weapons and come down to live peaceably with everyone else without fighting, because God does not want his people to kill one another all the time. You will live all right and not want for anything; you will always get what you ask for. So I gave up the study of law and took up the study of the Bible, and went to all the Christian revivals and missionary meetings.

I needed $90.00 to pull through the next school term, which would be over in June. I called on the churches for a donation of that amount, and Professor McCarty assured me that he would give me a certificate so that I could teach and pay back any amount loaned to me. The pastor said, "Yes, but the trustees of the church will meet on May 15, and if they decide to loan that to you, Mr. Burns, then I will surely approve it." But I needed the money right away. I had only $20.00 to my name.

So I have come to the conclusion that most all supposed Christian men and women are all talk, making promises that they cannot or will not fulfill. They say they will pray for you, but not in their hearts.

I went to Professor McCarty and told him what the pastor had said. He said, "I'm sorry, Mr. Burns." I said that I might as well leave and go to work, and he said, "Well, you have gotten a good education, I can say that much for you, and I can write out your certificate, and if you can find no other work you can present this certificate to school officials and they will find you a school in which to become a teacher. You have gone up very fast in your studies, and I have often told other people about how wonderfully fast you pick up in all the branches of study you have undertaken, leaving your white classmates far behind." So he wrote me a long set of letters and the certificate.

I got on the train to Atchison, and when I got there I telegraphed my old friend Major John J. Upham of the Fifth Cavalry, who was enlisting men at Leavenworth to go west. I told him that I was going to either Leavenworth or Lawrence to look for work. He told me to come ahead, and when I got to Leavenworth he was on the platform. He shook my hand and led me to his team a little way off, and took me in his buggy over to his house and bid me stay a few days. I stayed with him, and he took me around to the places where the soldiers drilled. Some men in the company knew me from the campaigns of

1876, and out on the shooting range Major Upham told the rest of the soldiers that I had served in the Sitting Bull War. A mark was placed at three hundred yards, and the major shot at it three times and hit it once. He handed me the gun. The first shot I hit near the bull's eye, and the second was just off the edge of the bull's eye, and on the third I was a little too high. But I had shot much better than the major, and he said, "Mike, you can shoot yet!" I had not shot for nearly ten years. Some of the officers said, "If he comes out to practice every day like these soldiers he can beat old Carver, Major!" "Yes, we would do well to send him to the front!"

We went home to our usual dinner. Major Upham always had a bottle of champagne at the table. The next morning I told my old friend that I was going down to Lawrence to work the hay harvest and would probably be gone a month or so. I told him that I would let him know what I was doing when I finished. He said, "All right. By all means let me hear from you. If you have no success in finding work, then let me know it soon, because there is some talk of enlisting quite a number of Indian scouts, and I would be willing to get you in." Then before I left his house he handed me a twenty-dollar bill, and he said, "If you do not find work soon, you can have that much at hand until you do."

So I went to Lawrence. The next day I got to a place and raked hay, and in a few days I stacked the hay close to the barn, and then I went out harrowing the cornfield. I stayed only three weeks, because I heard that near there was a US Indian school called Haskell, so I went over and met the superintendent. He told me that he wanted me to enter the school as a student, but I said, "I will join this school, not as a student but as a teacher." The superintendent said, "Oh, no, I can't enroll an Indian as a teacher when he first comes to school." I showed him my certificate. He said, "I'll have to refer this to the headquarters for Indian schools in the department in Washington."

"Well," I said, "if you're going to have to go to that much trouble I'll be on my way, for I am also a laborer and need to find work." I stayed about a week. I have nothing against the school for hospitality, and I was very kindly treated by the faculty. They said they were very sorry I could not stay with them, but I said I would not do so as a student.

Finally they took me back to town, and I took the train to Leavenworth. Major Upham told me that some recruits were going to take some horses to Caldwell, Kansas, and from there to Fort Reno, in the Indian Territory. He said, "I think you should go along. I'll take you over to General Miles's headquarters, and he and I will sign a recommendation to the commanding officer at Fort Reno to enlist you as a scout." He added, "I think that will suit you all right."

17

So I went with the horses, riding off on a freight train to Caldwell. I arrived there in the evening. The next day the horses were ready for the march to the front, and we reached Fort Reno in three days. There were Cheyenne and Arapahos from the Darlington Agency, which was about three and a half miles from the fort. They looked me over. The next day a schoolboy came up in a buggy and told me to get in. We drove around, down to the Indian camps, and I got off and was shown how to enter a lodge.

I went in, and there were many old Indian men and women inside. They raised their heads and looked at me for a moment, and then they all began to cry and sat close beside me, saying that it had been fifteen years since they had seen me. They said that at one time the soldiers fought them and captured many of their children, and I was one of them. One old woman came up and felt my ears and found a hole. She said that her daughter had pierced that hole when I was a baby. She was killed by soldiers at that fight, and I was taken.

The way they got to believe I was one of them was this: when I was at Fort Brown, Wyoming, I learned a few words of Arapaho, and I could use sign language, too. So when I arrived at Fort Reno I signaled to some of the Indians that I knew a little Arapaho. Still, they got the number of years down pretty exactly. While I was in that hut, though, I was thinking about how in the world I was going to get out of there so that I could go to the fort and enlist in the scouts.

The government wanted to enlist about five hundred scouts at the time, which was just when some cattlemen started to make trouble in the Territory. They had been cutting the fence surrounding the reservation so that they could drive their cattle across it without having to go across to Kansas City, which saved them about 125 miles. They drove about sixty thousand cattle across the reservation, using violence and not listening to orders. The agent at Darlington sent

Indian policemen with orders for them to leave, but the cattle boss just tore the orders up and told the policemen to hurry back the way they came or else they would be shot on the spot. There must have been five thousand cattlemen who defied the government's orders, and, the Indians reported, the cowboys always shot at them. Even when soldiers from Fort Reno accompanied the policemen, the cattlemen ordered them all back over the hills, telling them not to show their heads anywhere in sight. The soldiers returned to the fort and told the commanding officer, who reported to General Miles at Fort Leavenworth, who reported to the War Department in Washington, saying that a few regiments of soldiers ought to be sent out there, and at least five hundred Indian scouts.

I finally got to the fort. Three hundred Indians had enlisted, and my name was put in with the next lot. There were no objections to my enlistment after I laid down the letters from General Miles and Major Upham. I was ordered to report to Lieutenant Rice, who was detailed to take fifty Cheyenne and Arapaho scouts out. Lieutenant Rice also wanted a young man who could tend to his horse and fix things up around his place, extra work but also extra pay—I was going to get $25.00 a month from the government, and another $15.00 from him.

The soldiers were in great excitement all around the fort. Reports had come about cattlemen from Texas and their cowboys, all classes of men: there were Mexicans, and half-breeds, and very rough white men from Texas and New Mexico and southern Arizona, and there were about five thousand of them, and they wanted to make trouble with the government.

The next evening the fifty scouts I was among were ordered to get ready to march the next morning up the Canadian River to Camp Supply. I had no horse, and I hurried around to get one. There was a Cheyenne boy, a classmate of mine, named Tom Roberts who brought a pony over and asked for $25.00. I paid him and bought a secondhand saddle for $12.00.

We set off, marching for three long days to get to Camp Supply. I recognized the country everywhere we went, since I had come there in 1875, about ten years earlier, when we were on our way north to fight the Sioux. But we didn't stay there; instead, we were ordered to march south to Fort Elliott, Texas. Now we were commanded by Lieutenant Black, whom I worked for instead of Lieutenant Rice.

It took us four days to get to Fort Elliott. We were there for a couple of weeks when word came back from where we had come from, Fort Reno, that a large number of Cheyenne and Arapahos had left the reservation and were making their way south. We were ordered out toward Fort Sill, but we didn't see any sign of the Indians. The cowboys out there had been threatening the soldiers and demanding provisions, which the soldiers gave them. Finally we headed toward Fort Reno and found an Indian camp, probably within fifty miles of Fort Elliott. Lieutenant Black ordered us to escort the Indians back to their homes. We took 150 lodges of Cheyenne and Arapahos to Fort Elliott, which must have been about seven hundred people. Their chief's name was Crazy Mule, a Cheyenne. The commanding officer wanted to find out where they were going, so he asked if I could understand their language. I told him that I could not talk to them right out, but that I could understand the motions of their hands. He said that that would do, and so the next morning I went with Crazy Mule's people up to headquarters. Major Mills, the commanding officer, asked why they had left the reservation without permission, and Crazy Mule answered that he just wanted to go hunt antelope and deer and buffalo, for winter was coming. He had not harmed anyone, he said, but if he were on the warpath he could kill anyone who found him.

Major Mills ordered Crazy Mule back to the reservation, dispatching twenty-five soldiers and fifteen Indian scouts to go with them, saying that if they encountered any cattlemen they were to make them detour off the reservation and arrest them if they refused. The grass in that part of the country was very tall and wet, and it was close to fall, and every morning I had gone out to gather feed for the horses and gotten soaked. I got sick, because I wasn't used to such a climate. I was worse off than anyone in camp and had to go to the camp hospital.

While I was there I wrote to my old friend General George Crook, who was now stationed at Fort Bowie, Arizona, leading a campaign against the Chiricahua Apaches, whose chief was called Geronimo. I said that I was with people who were strangers to me, and in a low and damp country, which was hard on me. I was always coughing, and I could hardly be heard when I spoke to anyone. If I stayed two or three months more, I said, I might see the end of my days. I asked him to use his influence to transfer me out to the Department of Arizona, since he knew me well and knew that I was an Apache.

I stayed around the post on the sick list, taking medicine every morning. The more medicine I took the worse I got, so I concluded that the medicine was no good. I got some herbs from the Indians.

In less than three weeks a telegram came, and the commanding officer told me to sell my stuff, since I was to go at once to Dodge City, Kansas, and from there to Fort Leavenworth. This must have been in October. I sold my saddle and horse and left word for Lieutenant Black to send me $15.00 for a pistol I had loaned him. Then I rode off to Camp Supply, where I was very surprised to find my old friend H. S. Bishop, who was now a captain of the Fifth Cavalry. My stage out didn't leave until 7:00 the next morning, so I stayed overnight in his quarters, and we talked quite a bit about the old days of the Sioux War, staying up most of the night and promising to write so that we could share one another's misfortunes and happiness.

The next morning he made me breakfast, and then took me to the post office. He held my hand and said, "Be good by all means, my boy. Perhaps we will never meet again, but nevertheless be good as long as you may live." We said good-bye, and soon the stage was out of sight of the camp.

We crossed the river, and passed over the hills, and then I looked back and saw the valleys of Beaver and Wolf Creeks, which join together at the Canadian River. I have come to the conclusion that the mind of man changes, but the country never changes.

The road to the railroad was about ninety-five miles. It took the stage all day and night to get there, and we rolled into Dodge City at about 9:00 in the morning. I went to the telegraph office and sent a telegram to my old friend Major Upham, then got aboard a train for Kansas City and there changed to go to Fort Leavenworth. When I reached the fort, Major Upham met me and took me to his quarters, where I slept soundly for the first time in six months. At ten the next morning he took me to General Miles's office. We found him sitting there, and he bade us come in and be seated. In a few minutes he pulled out a letter that General Crook had written to him from Fort Bowie, Arizona, and he asked me if it was true that I wanted to be transferred out of his department. I said it was. He said, "Where do you want to go?" I said I wanted to go out to Arizona, where I could join the scouts going after the Chiricahua Apaches. He asked me where my home was, and I answered that it was the San Carlos Agency. "Well, sir," he said, "I can only send you as far as my department extends, that is, to Fort Bayard, New Mexico, and from there you can go out with some scouting parties, and when you find it, you can join General Crook's command again." I said that would be acceptable, and that was in fact just what I had been planning to do. "Very well," he said. "Be ready in the morning. The quartermaster will have everything ready for you. You will go to Kansas City, then to Albuquerque, then to Deming, and then change trains for Silver City, and there will be a light wagon there going on to Fort Bayard. Report to the commanding officer there for duty."

So I got on the train and did as General Miles directed. I reached Fort Bayard on October 15, 1885. There were only a few soldiers around, since most of them were off looking for Geronimo and his band of warriors. I was there a few weeks, quartered by myself where a whole company used to stay, when some soldiers came back with a sick man. They made his bed in the bunk next to mine. He looked as if he would die at any moment, and that night he did die. He had not showed up for breakfast, and the cook was mad because he had had to cook for more than one person. He howled at the dead man, "Are you dead asleep, or dead entirely?" He went up and shook the man, but he was sound dead, so stiff that he could be carried like a log. I was sleeping there only two feet away from him, but nothing bothered me anymore.

The sergeant reported that the man had died of unknown causes, and there was a funeral for the soldier that afternoon, and the poor young man was laid away in honor.

There was still a company of cavalry and another of infantry at the fort, to protect it from depredations by outlaws and Indians. A few weeks later a report came that a party of Indians had come into a little town north of Fort Bayard, killed three men, and driven off several animals. The commanding officer ordered a company of cavalry and me to go out to see what had happened. That afternoon we marched over the mountains to a little place called Miner's Pass, where nearly every house was a saloon, and the soldiers would drop out of line to go off and get a few bottles of beer or whiskey.

We made camp at the bottom of the mountains, and that night the soldiers got to fighting among themselves. Some went and got their guns, but they were taken away from them. The next day these men were stripped of their arms and horses and had to walk. We followed a creek and came to a piney valley, where we made another camp. We passed many ranches along the way, but it seems they hadn't had any trouble.

We went on the next morning, traveling five or seven miles along a brushy canyon whose sides were lined with small pine trees. I was riding alongside the column. All at once I noticed the commanding officer stop, and I thought that he must have noticed Indians in the distance. I went up and the officer called to me, "You go a little off the hillside and see what that is up yonder. It looks to me like a bear standing on its hind feet listening to our marching." So I went off with my gun in my arms, ready to shoot at any minute. I peeped over the hill, covering my head with some brush. I could plainly see that old bear, but it was just an old stump, a pine tree burned down to half its size. From a distance, it looked like a man standing. I motioned the soldiers to move forward, and when they had got to where I was they all began to laugh, saying that it really did look like an old bear on its hind feet. So when they all got it settled in their minds that there was no bear, they started to march again.

We came to a cattle ranch, where the owner appeared with a gun in his hand. The commander asked him if he knew anything about Chiricahuas raiding the valley. The man said no, there hadn't been any Indians around, but five or seven miles up the creek some cowboys and miners had got into a fight. He said, "I wouldn't expect any Chiricahuas in this country." It was true, too, for the Chiricahuas would not come this far north, to country they did not know, for where they traveled they knew every foothill and every waterhole.

So we continued our marching until we came to some deserted houses, out of one of which came three or four men armed with pistols. The commander asked them if they had seen or heard any Indians, and they said no, but some cowboys had come around and shot the place up and come near to killing some of them. The cowboys had run off in every direction, they added. The commanding officer asked whether their statements were true about there being no Indians, and the miners said, "We swear to our statements. We know nothing about any Indians near here."

The command marched off to a nice clear creek running a little way away, with all kinds of shade trees. The commander told the soldiers to eat dinner and then go around to see whether they could find any bodies, or any signs of Indians coming through.

They never did find any. I think what happened was that the prospectors held their ground against the cowboys, and the cowboys rode down to Fort Bayard to blame the attack on the Indians. This has been done many times in the past. White renegades and Mexicans were always blaming the Indians. When Geronimo was 250 miles away from the Chiricahua Mountains down in Mexico, white men wanted to make legal claims for damages, and so they got together and hired some smart lawyers, and they made claims for a few rough old houses that cowboys had burned down. Everything was done by the Indians, they said, no matter who really did the deed. If the government officials had taken the time to make an inquiry throughout that country I might have been some help, with no guesswork about it. But lots of supposedly honest government officials did many dishonest things for a little side money. No, I am too honest to become one of those persons.

We scared around everywhere, looking for signs of Indians, and then we tried to see if we could come across the cowboys, but we saw only horse tracks on the run. It looked as if there had been ten or fifteen men on horseback. The trail separated, with some of the men going off toward Albuquerque. One of the sergeants said that it wouldn't be any use following the tracks any farther, because this affair had been done a week before, and the fellows who carried out the attack might be all the way down in old Mexico by now.

We went back to camp, and the commander asked me what I thought. I said that I believed that cowboys had done these things, because there were no signs of Indians anywhere. He said, "Well, there's no use in us fooling around here, then, pretending that we're on the trail of hostile Indians. There's no Indians in this part of the country. We'll make for the post in the morning."

So the next morning we marched back the way we came, and as we did I started shooting at some quail off in the bushes. I knocked several down from my horse, and the soldiers and officers said that they had never seen anybody shoot birds off their seats like that Indian with the rifle, adding, "I wouldn't like to have him after me."

We arrived back at camp, and almost as soon as we arrived the soldiers were ordered to the front. On November 27, 1885, two companies of the Sixth Cavalry went to Separ, a station on the Southern Pacific Railroad. I went with them to join twenty-five Apache scouts who were going out after Geronimo. It had been reported that Geronimo's men had killed six soldiers near Lordsburg, about thirty-five miles west of Separ. The two companies went down and camped below Silver City, a very rough mining town. For once the soldiers didn't go into town to get whiskey. They behaved themselves, and the next morning we were off on the desert road toward the railroad. Some of the soldiers said that they would like to come across a gang of Chiricahuas so that they would see what I would do. Another soldier said, "You ought to see the way he kills birds while they're flying. He'll make it hot for the Chiricahuas if he sees any." So the others stopped making fun of me. They didn't know that I was an Apache myself, nor did I tell them, lest they be afraid of me.

The little command arrived at the railroad station at about four in the afternoon. Toward evening some more soldiers came down from the mountains, and with them came five Apache scouts. The next morning more soldiers arrived, rolling in on the train from El Paso, and there were twenty Tonto Apache scouts with them. Lieutenant Ship, who was in charge of the scouts, told me to go with a group of soldiers who were going out into the field, but I told him that I was supposed to go on through to Bowie Station with the twenty-five scouts who were going back to the San Carlos Agency to be discharged there. He said, "Do as you are ordered." I went to the telegraph office and asked the operator to send a telegram to General Crook asking him to counter Lieutenant Ship's orders. I had only one month left to serve and didn't like the thought of going out into the field for no telling how long.

About two hours later a telegram arrived. General Crook said to show it to Lieutenant Ship. It had my orders to proceed to the San Carlos Agency. Lieutenant Ship didn't read it through; he just told me to go where I wanted to go, and not long afterward I was on the train with the Tonto Apache scouts. I could talk only with the ones who understood some English; I was just as bad off among the Indians as a white man.

The train arrived at Bowie that afternoon. The Indian scouts went to work unloading their stuff and made some supper, and the next morning they got ready to travel overland to Solomonville on foot. I got ready, too, but the officer in charge wanted me to go with the supplies to Fort Bowie. I tried to make him understand that I was on my way to San Carlos and was to remain there until my discharge. But he said no, I would have to go to Fort Bowie. I was in the same fix as at Separ. So I went in and sent another telegram to General Crook. I got one back and took it to the officer, who said, "Well, get ready to move on with the others right away." We were issued five days' rations, and we moved on. The little company moved about twenty miles that day. There were two little mule wagons that went along to carry the grub and the scouts' belongings. I wasn't used to traveling so much on foot, but the sergeant in charge—there always had to be a white man in charge wherever we went—was a kind-hearted fellow and let me climb into the wagon with him.

We made Solomonville in two days. The next day we were supposed to camp at a little town about twenty-two miles below on the Gila River called Pina. The sergeant told the Indian scouts not to stray too far away from the wagon, because the Mormons would shoot at them in the country through which we were now traveling, where Geronimo had crossed the river and shot many white men. They would take them to be hostiles, since some white people look upon the Indians all alike. Whether they were Tontos, or Mojaves, or Yumas, or Coyoteros, or San Carlos, they were all Chiricahuas to the Mormons.

Some of the scouts went far ahead all the same, and the whites noticed them and got guns and came out to shoot them. The scouts ran back to the wagons, and the sergeant again explained the facts to them. He told them that they ought to know by now that almost all the white settlements in the Southwest were deadly enemies to the Apaches, and that white people wanted to shoot Indians when they saw them. He told them to march close to the wagons until we got close to Fort Thomas, where we got two more days' rations. Then we went down to the Gila River and camped at an old deserted agency, where the wagon road crosses the one that goes up to Fort Apache. The reservation line was close to Fort Thomas, and after we passed it the scouts knew that there would be no more trouble from the whites, only from the Chiricahuas, maybe. It was only twenty-three miles to the agency, and we got there about two o'clock. That afternoon there were a lot of Indian men around, and I found out later that there was a recruiting drive going on to raise another 150 scouts, since news had come that the Chiricahuas had killed four Mojaves out in the field. They were the first to volunteer against Geronimo.

I hadn't seen my own people for nearly fifteen years until that day. Nobody knew me, nor did I know any of them. People were looking at me, though, asking among themselves who I was. Then one of them came right up to me and called me by my Indian name, Hoomothya, Wet Nose. He was a cousin of mine. It is wonderful that Indians have such good memories. We had been separated for at least twenty years, since we were small children, but this Indian recognized me as soon as he saw me. His named was Quaknidueyah, Summer Deer. He told me that his parents had been killed by the Maricopas and Pimas when he was just a baby, and he had been carried away by some older relatives who escaped. He went to Carlisle, and when he came back to San Carlos he was James Roberts.

18

There were some white soldiers at the agency, and the sergeant made arrangements for me to draw rations with them. I unloaded my little bundle into a tent near a large wall tent where the soldiers had their dining room. That afternoon a captain I used to know came along— Captain John G. Bourke of the Third Cavalry, who was still the aide-de-camp to General Crook. He was much surprised to see me, as much as the Indians were on my arrival at the San Carlos Agency. This was on about December 5, 1885.

I was once more on my mother's land. I was hoping that a close cousin of mine whose name is Cealiah, Worthless, was around. As for the rest of my family, well, I have already said what happened to them, and there's no use saying anything more: my mother was killed by US soldiers somewhere about 1869, and my father was killed, also by soldiers with Pimas and Maricopas, in a cave on the Salt River in the winter of 1872.

When I got to the agency there were about a hundred and fifty Mojave and Tonto Apaches serving as scouts with Al Sieber, who was the chief of scouts under General Crook. There were another two hundred and fifty scouts out in the field fighting the Chirica-huas with the US soldiers. When I got there the men, women, and children were gathering up for a war dance, and I was anxious to see this, since I hadn't seen an Apache dance for so many years. The night came, and a fire was lit, and the Indians collected. The dancers were naked, with just some strings and feathers on their bodies, and they carried guns. They danced forward, some of them running around in circles. Women went in and out among the men. They kept this dance up all night, and before daylight the men were on the road, going to war. The older men kept on singing until the sun was up, and then the Indians went home, lonely for their young men, the fathers and mothers grieving. But they dared not cry, for that was bad luck. They had to bear it in their hearts. The only thing to do was cheer for their success, and to come back victorious and with plenty of spoils from the enemy.

During the day I had no duties, so I wandered around the Mojave Apache camp, the tribe I belonged to, but I could not speak to them in their tongue except through an interpreter, just like a white man. I found many Indians in the camp, but they did not know me. At one camp an old man said he was my father, but I knew better than to say that I was his son.

The next day some women and children came along, and as soon as they saw me they called my name, and said I was the one who had been captured. I said that was true, and a woman with four children said that she had escaped alive out of that very cave where our families were slaughtered. She was spared, because she and five other women were away that morning gathering mescal. That day I met my cousin who had married the son of a noted chief of the Verde River band of Mojave Apaches. His name was Jutahamaka, Swift Hawk, and he became a great medicine man, too. He was not there, since he too had enlisted in the scouts and was among the group that had just gone out. He was supposed to be back in two months.

More and more Indians recognized me as the one who had been taken away, and they often cried when they saw me, because it made them think of old times. It was as if I were a ghost come back to them from the dead, dressed in different clothes.

I stayed with a detachment of the Eleventh Cavalry, Captain Pierce's company. He was the acting agent at San Carlos. When the company was ordered back to Fort Elliott, I moved in with the Indian company, invited to do so by an Indian named Captain Snook, who was the first sergeant.

On January 26, 1886, I was discharged from the US Army. Afterward I went to the Indians across the river, about half a mile from the agency, where my cousin lived. She had five children, three grown girls and two small boys. Her husband was still out scouting.

I had a hard time getting the money that was owed to me for traveling from Fort Reno, a distance of about 1,100 miles. One of the army officers said that Indians never got paid for mileage, and he would not approve any money for me. I wrote a letter to General Crook asking that I get my allowance, and two months later a letter came telling me to go to Fort Thomas and get my payment. The distance was about thirty miles, and when I arrived I collected $97.00, gladly signing for it.

Captain Pierce called me in and asked me what kind of work I could do. I told him I could do rough carpentry, painting, and some farming, too. So he put me on the list as a carpenter to repair a schoolhouse for $2.50 a day, and then he put me to work recruiting children to attend the school, which had been closed for nearly three years on account of the Chiricahua war. I went around to the different camps urging the old folks to send the children to school, because education is the making of a man and woman. Some of the old people refused, claiming that some of their children had been sent back east; they were supposed to be gone for three years, but it was going on six years since they had seen them. Some of the older children were willing to come to school, though, so we collected nearly fifty students, all boys. Some of the boys were willing to have their hair cut, but others refused until the boys who were willing made enough fun of them that the others finally cut their hair, too.

A young man named Robert McIntosh had charge of the San Carlos, Tonto, White Mountain, and Coyotero Apaches. I was in charge of the Mojave and Yuma Apache boys.

Not long afterward came a man named Mr. Watkins, the superintendent, with his daughter, a schoolteacher. We got along very well until news came that a band of Geronimo's was going to raid the agency. Most of the children ran away, and the school was closed for the rest of the year.

Robert McIntosh went back to his camp along the Gila River. He was a son-in-law of Eskiminzin, the Aravaipa Apache war chief, who fought his way out when his people were massacred at old Fort Grant. He often related that he had killed at least fifty Pimas and Maricopas.

The Pinal and Aravaipa Apaches had come in to Fort Grant somewhere around 1869 to make their home near the post so that the soldiers would protect them. They were told to make their camp across Aravaipa Creek about half a mile from the garrison. While the Apaches were dancing that night they were surrounded by Pimas, Maricopas, and some Mexicans and white men from Tucson, and most all of the Apaches were shot down. Eskiminzin concealed his gun, and when the soldiers came to take the surviving Apaches to the post he escaped and told his family to run away. The Pimas chased him, but he shot them at close range right and left. He had an old Henry rifle with eight shots, so every time he fired he killed five or six men. He said he had captured this old gun in the Rincon Mountains, where the Apaches had jumped a Mexican camp, killed several men, and captured a few children.

If the soldiers at Fort Grant had made any attempt to stop the invaders from Tucson, the massacre would never have happened. The massacre happened right in sight of the soldiers. Afterward, no Apache would dare go near any white man's camp to make a treaty.

Word came to the agency for the chiefs to bring their able-bodied young men to enlist to become scouts, with Mari-hildero as the chief of scouts, and his nephews Antonio and Gabaritto as interpreters. This is what Little Jack—his Indian name was Mothawha, Wind— told me, anyway. Twenty-five Mojave Apaches and fifty other Apaches from various groups joined two companies of the Fifth Cavalry on a six-month enlistment. I joined, too. The command marched down the Gila River and then up the San Pedro to the old military road to Tucson. The next day we reached Tucson. The command remained at Fort Lowell to get fitted out, and then we were ordered to march eastward. We crossed the San Pedro again, and in a couple of days we could plainly see the mountains where the Chiricahuas camped, just a few miles from Fort Bowie. We had to cross a waterless desert to make the mountains, where there was some chance of finding water. Some soldiers were left behind with the pack mules, and they got lost, so some of us Indians were ordered to go back and shoot our guns so that the pack train could find us. Five men were picked to go, along with one soldier. Late at night, finally, the mule train came along with our grub and some blankets, and the next morning we cooked up a breakfast.

Afterward we marched out to climb the rough mountains, and we came near Fort Bowie. We Indians were told not to go near the post, because the soldiers were on the watch for Indians and would shoot on sight. The Indian scouts were told to wear red cloths on their heads and to follow the columns of soldiers, and in this way we reached the fort and stayed there for five or six days. The command-ing officer said that he had heard nothing about the Chiricahua chiefs coming in to talk, but he said that if Cochise were alive they would have come in—if, that is, they were assured of being treated justly. When his people were called in to a meeting with the soldiers they were shot down, so Cochise wanted to be assured of just treatment.

In the spring of 1887 the Apache Kid turned up at the San Carlos Agency. He belonged to a band called the Pinal Apaches, who ranged from the Sierra Anchas to the Graham Mountains along the ranges east of the San Pedro River, and especially around Aravaipa Canyon. I remember that he had a stepfather who once killed two men, and he was to be killed too, but he ran off with another band of Apaches until everyone came into the San Carlos Agency. Then, guarded by soldiers, he came in and was spared his life for a time. But there was a brother yet, and he had been waiting for a chance to get even for a long time.

Al Sieber, who was chief of scouts, raised the Kid. Sieber allowed him to join the soldiers, as young as he was, just able to carry a gun. That was why he was called the Kid, on account of his always being the youngest around. He was a man when I saw him, with two brothers and two sisters. Both of the brothers had been killed above the agency, on the Gila River, after the Kid had killed some relatives of the killers. That is just the way it is: someone takes the life of someone else for something that happened years ago.

The Kid was now first sergeant of scouts. One fine morning he and six of his men were out visiting their old camps on the Gila River, about six miles above the agency. The camp was on the north side of the river, and on the south side there were Apache Mojave and Apache Yuma camps, and then a couple of Aravaipa and Pinal Apache camps. The chief of the Aravaipa camp was Eskinaspas, and there was another chief called Poulgatatehaw, which means Thorny Head. His brother, the Apache Kid's stepfather, had killed a man a long time ago, and a relative of the dead man had been threatening to kill the chief in revenge. The chief told his friends that the would-be killer was a Mojave. He hid himself safely away in camp all day. About a week later there was a great commotion in his camp, and we heard shots being fired and then saw several men racing their horses over the hills. They got down to a little gulch, and then more shots were fired. This went on all afternoon, and when the shooting finally stopped we heard much crying. Some of the men came over to our camp and said that Poulgatatehaw had been shot dead, and that the

Mike Burns in uniform during his service as an Indian scout.

Kid and five scouts had gone out after the man who had killed him. The chief's band moved into the agency for protection, and hardly anybody stayed out at the old camp.

Instead of going back to the agency, the Apache Kid and his scouts went over toward the San Pedro River, following Aravaipa Canyon to the mouth, where four or five families, relatives of the killer, had their fields. The killer's stepfather was out working among his corn, pumpkins, and watermelons when the Kid came by. The Kid called him over. The man hadn't heard anything about what had happened, but still the Kid shot him dead and told the rest of the people there to leave. Then he threw the dead man into his tepee and set it on fire.

The Kid's gang then went up to Table Mountain, where there was a little gulch above which was a meadow surrounded by walnut and sycamore trees and some pines. There was a white man in the field working. Someone in the party said something in English to him, telling him that they had some news for him. When he came over, an Indian shot the man dead. They all went into the dead man's house and got all the grub they wanted, as well as three good saddle horses. Then they set the house on fire.

The next day the gang went across Aravaipa Creek and climbed the Pinaleño Mountains, where they could look up and down the whole Gila Valley. Then they descended and crossed the Gila near Fort Thomas and traveled along the river about twenty-five miles above the agency.

There was a half-breed Mexican and Apache man who belonged to the Kid's band. Captain Pierce sent him to tell the Kid and the rest of his gang that if they came quietly to the agency they would not be punished very hard, just put in the guardhouse for a few months. Just as the half-breed was delivering this offer, a great earthquake hit, and all the Indian people felt the shock. It made the Indians think that the world was coming to an end. A medicine man told them to gather all the Indians together at a certain camp and start dancing and keep going for a full thirty days, when God would appear to them and re-store all their land to the red men. The white men would vanish from the Indians' land, and all the dead Indians would come back to life and join their relatives, and no Indian would ever die again.

A middle-aged man named Echawamahu, Enemy Head, at the San Carlos Agency was a Yavapai and used to roam in the Bradshaw,

Bill Williams, and San Francisco Mountains and the Black Hills. He came down with his people when they were moved from the Verde River at General Crook's orders in 1873. He was a lonely man and had no relatives, and he started acting strange. He would go off for the whole day, and then come back and eat only green grass, and maybe some flowers that he had gathered, but he would refuse the food that was cooked for him. For a month he would leave camp before anyone was up and return and go to bed before anyone saw him. Whenever anyone did see him, he was looking up at the sky. Everybody started worrying about him. A man named Shaihaw went to Echawamahu and asked him what was the matter, since he never wanted to eat anything. Echawamahu replied that he wasn't hungry, his stomach was always full, the Great Spirit gave him all the food he needed. Shaihaw was astonished. Then Echawamahu told him to bring everyone else at sunrise, and he would have more to say.

Shaihaw gathered the Indians and took them to see Echawamahu. He gave instructions that the group should be made up of the members of four camps, each coming from a different direction. They should be led by four young people, two young men and two young women, each carrying a cross on which was tied a white cloth. At the center of the cross there had to be a looking glass. Behind these four young persons must be two young men beating a small drum, and then all the people in their best clothes. They had to come to Echawamahu's camp in four directions, and when they approached they had to send in four young maidens dressed in white, each with white eagle feathers in their hair and fastened to their shoulders. The maidens would sprinkle dust between their fingers and make signs over the assembled people, and daub him in dust, and then the medicine man would paint his face yellow. No one was to touch him.

It took all day to perform this act. Echawamahu told them that he had seen great things, and that he had gone to another world and come back, led by the Great Spirit. He was sent back, he said, to tell the people that great things were about to happen. The world was going to change, and if all the Indians listened and acted with one heart, then God would restore their land and set a plague loose on the white people, and they would disappear. Now the Indians had to dance, beginning at sunset, all through the night, and to send word throughout the San Carlos Agency for all the young men to do the same.

Some young men carried this news to a Tonto camp at Coyote Hole, about nine miles west of the agency, halfway to Globe. The whole camp broke up and moved toward the agency, to Charlie Pan's camp, where a big medicine dance would be held. The chief there was named Ejachtashunha, Big Hat. Echawamahu was there, sitting in the center next to the fire, and everyone saluted him when they walked by. I didn't get close enough to make a bow to the supposed great medicine man, but I heard that anyone who was there who didn't believe would cause the whole dance to fail, so in order for it to succeed, our hearts had to be strong in believing that this great change would come.

Every now and again the dancing would stop, and the four young men and women would go around the crowd putting something on everyone's forehead as a token. They began with the medicine man. I was getting tired and was with some boys from the school, so we went home, even though we had been told not to leave until sunup.

There was another dance the next week at a Mojave camp whose chief was Marshall Pete. I went but didn't care to dance. There were several pretty girls who came up and asked me to, and finally they dragged me out. I was slow keeping time with the beating drums, and the maidens pushed me along. Afterward I wanted to go back to my gang, but I was kept there in the middle of the ring. At midnight the men fired a volley into the air as a sign of joy, and then the dancing continued. I tried every way I could to get away, but the girls grabbed hold of my arms, and I was kept there nearly all night. My shirt was torn to strings.

The next day all the Indians went home. This was in May 1887, and it was getting to be very hot, and dusty, and salty. None of what the medicine man said came true. Maybe it was because there were doubtful hearts in the midst. The earthquake came only a few weeks afterward, and that startled the doubtful Indians, since something wonderful did indeed occur, just as the medicine man had said. So again many people turned their belief toward Echawamahu.

Captain Pierce was now employing me as an assistant farmer under a farmer for the Mojaves whose name was Dr. Paughborn. I was still staying with my cousin. Word came that the Indians were gathering for more dancing to bring the world to an end, and that those who didn't come would be punished like the white men when it did. Dr. Paughborn asked me every day whether I wanted to go to Coyote Hole and join the dancers. I told him that I didn't care, come what may. If the world came to an end and everything perished, I didn't believe that I would be spared.

I stayed with him for about a week until Captain Pierce sent word for me to come up to the agency and work as an interpreter, at the usual $2.50 a day. That suited me pretty well, since I just had to sit in a chair, there not being many Indians around for whom I had to interpret. I was at the agency for about a week, watching as families came in to draw their rations.

The Apache Kid and his gang, now numbering about ten others, were still at large. Some of the people came down from Coyote Hole and camped across the river from us. I found out they were going up the San Carlos River into the mountains, where there was to be a great dance at Cassadore's camp. This old San Carlos chief had an orchard of peaches for sale, and everyone from Coyote Hole wanted to go get some. Some of the young men caught a pony for me to ride, and we went off at a fast gait. The distance was about twelve miles. We got there at dusk, and we could hear the drums beating from a good distance away. We tied our ponies to thick brush when we arrived, then went to watch the dance begin.

All of a sudden we heard gunshots. We didn't pay much attention until someone came by and said that the Apache Kid was shooting at anyone who crossed his path. We were going that way, and we heard more shots fired, and they sounded pretty close, too, so everybody was ready to leave, and in a few minutes my friends had all gone. I turned to go back to where I had tied my horse, and when I got there it was frightened and jumpy, and it had pulled so hard on the rope that I couldn't get it loose. There was a man nearby, and I asked him if he had a knife. He said yes, and handed me the knife, and I cut my pony loose. The man had ridden away, but I overtook him and returned the knife.

There had to have been at least fifteen hundred Indians there, and they were all scared of a party of eleven men. I had nothing to protect myself with, but most of the other Indians were armed. We passed down the river, and as we went along people begged to ride along with us for protection. I was advised not to listen to their entreaties but to look out for myself—the best policy. Even so, we soon turned into a big crowd.

We got home at midnight. The next morning, we found Indians everywhere, hiding in the thick brush. We laughed at one another for the great escape we had made the previous night, especially when we found out that the Kid wasn't anywhere in the country; instead, a bunch of Indians drunk on tizwin with whiskey mixed in had done the shooting. Some said that the people in Cassadore's band were tired of the crowds and wanted to chase people away, so they began shooting, saying that the bad Apache Kid was near. Many of the Indians had even abandoned their horses; some of the women from Coyote Hole walked all the way back, about fifteen miles.

Another week went by, and then word came that there would be another great dance at Coyote Hole. Every Indian was to be present, carrying firearms. The people were to come from the four directions, as before, and dance through the night. All the Indians—the Coyoteros, the Mojaves, the Yumas, the Tontos, the San Carlos, the Aravaipas, all the Apaches—were to gather at the fire and dance.

At midnight the medicine man ordered all the men to shoot their weapons, and he said that the bullets had melted away. So it would be when the whites came, he said: their bullets would melt away and not hit any Indians, but our guns would hit the soldiers. The Great Spirit would help the Indians, who would command the soldiers' guns to be useless. But the medicine man said don't worry, no one would bother us anyway as long as we were all together.

Captain Pierce had been in the service since West Point, and he was a thoughtful man. If he had been quick-tempered, he would have ordered the soldiers and scouts and Indian policemen to fire at the dancers. The farmers were complaining that there were no Indians to work the fields, but Captain Pierce said that this was their time to dance, and that they would come back when they got tired of dancing, since their legs would not last forever.

Indians did come in from Coyote Hole to draw rations of flour, sugar, coffee, and beans. After a while some came down from the medicine camp to stay in the agency, tired of being out in the sun all day, tired and hungry. They said that the people at Coyote Hole were starting to quarrel among themselves, and before long they would all break loose from Echawamahu's camp.

Before they moved from Coyote Hole, however, General Nelson Miles arrived at the agency and said that he wanted to see all the headmen. None of the chiefs could be found except Captain Coffee, the old Yuma chief, also called Coffee or Chief José. He asked General Miles for a written pass so that he could go off the reservation down to old Fort Yuma and visit his people at Palomas, Mohawk, and Agua Caliente.

In the meanwhile, runners had gone out to Coyote Hole to say that the big chief soldier had arrived at San Carlos, where he would command the campaign against the Chiricahuas. That frightened some of the families, who went back to the agency. The rest, though, dared the soldiers to come shoot them, saying that they had done nothing wrong and would not move from that place. They said that they were obeying the command of the Great Father in Heaven, and if they hadn't obeyed he would have been awfully hurt.

But, of course, the white people do not understand the way Indians serve their Great Spirit, or God. The white people have their books, and from the books they read about God, while the Indians only believe what has been commanded by the Great Spirit in their dreams. If they did not obey the medicine men, then God would be mad and not help them.

General Miles did not come to trouble the Indians. He listened to their appeals to find out what they wanted. He told me to send out a man in the night to tell the Indians to send their chiefs. At the time, these were Wapukadapa, Little Flat Block, who was chief of the Mojave B band; Makwa, Quail's Crest, the chief of the Mojave A band; Marshall Pete, the chief of the Mojave C band; Coquannathacka, Green Leaf, the chief of the Mojave E band; Paquala, Long Man, the chief of the Mojave D band; Kawpeteyu, Turtle Egg, the chief of the Mojave F band; Pachine; Poulthywcadedappa, Whitish Spots on His Forehead, the chief of the Mojave G band; and last Sygollah or Yaqkaquackcha, Crooked Mouth, who I suppose never followed anyone's advice and had his own ways. He was the chief of the Mojave H band. Snook was the chief of the Yuma B band, and Captain Coffee was the chief of the Yuma A band. The Yumas had only two bands. The Tontos had a lot of chiefs whose names I cannot remember, except that Charlie Pan was the head chief.

The man I sent went out to the medicine camp in the early morning. The crowd was still dancing, but a cry went up that a man was approaching on horseback. The man called out that the chiefs had to come to the agency before ten o'clock to have a talk with the great soldier chief, and to hear what the great General Nelson Miles had to say. Makwa did not go on account of being crippled and old, but he sent his nephew Waygahigha, Wet Back, to represent the Mojave A band. About noon the chiefs came together for the talk.

The Indians said that they were tired of being held prisoner for so long. They said that General Crook had told them that he wanted them to be examples to the other Apaches, and that when the other Apaches came down to farm on the bottomlands, the Mojaves and Yumas could go back to their homes in the Verde Valley. They would send their children to school, and they would work and show everyone that they wanted to be just like any other people in the land. General Crook said that this would take five or seven years and no longer, and that by all means in that time they must help the government fight any warlike Indians. If they did that, he said, then they would earn respect and get help.

General Miles replied that he was sorry, but General Crook had made promises that he could not keep. General Crook had no more power than any Indian, General Miles said. They could ask the Great White Father in Washington to do these things, of course, but General Crook may have already asked, and the Great White Father might have said no to General Crook's request for their return while Geronimo was making so much trouble for the people of Arizona and New Mexico. The people of Yavapai County and northwestern Arizona did not care to have them back in that part of the country, he added.

"It is too soon for you to be civilized," he said, "so that you could go back and live among those people whose animals and property you destroyed and stole. Nevertheless, it is true that you have been a great help to the government in the war against the Chiricahuas, and I do feel for your people. I will do all that I can to have you all sent back to your old homes, but I cannot say how long it will take to get an answer to my request from Washington. I have to send a long letter stating all that you have said to me about General Crook's great promises to you. I will add that almost all of you enlisted in the army to help fight the Chiricahuas."

The chiefs talked among themselves very forcefully, and then they said that if General Miles wasn't sure about General Crook's promises, he should send for General Crook to be present at the meeting. But General Miles told them to be at ease. He said that he wanted them to go out and select places where they wanted land, and they should do nothing but farm and attend to their livestock, and after a while they would be prosperous, just the same as white people. He would send a lieutenant with them to make sure that white people didn't make any trouble when they saw the Indians, thinking that they had broken out of the reservation and gone on the warpath. The lieutenant would go with them to Fort McDowell, and there they would look over the bottomlands, and he would write a report in his little book about what the Indians thought of the place, and about how many Indians could live there and farm the land.

Lieutenant Watson of the Tenth Cavalry was detailed to go with the Mojave and Tonto Apaches to Fort McDowell, and thence to follow the Rio Verde to Fort Whipple, and then across the desert to Fort Mohave and then Los Angeles, the headquarters of the Department of Pacific, which General Miles commanded. Captain Coffee, the Yuma chief, was to go to Willcox and get on a train for Los Angeles to meet General Miles.

General Miles selected me to go with Captain Coffee. He and another Indian by the name of Sam Kill got ready, and then an ambulance came and took us to Fort Grant. The next day another light wagon took us to the railroad station at Willcox. We arrived at about noon, and stayed in this rough little town until the train arrived about half past nine that night. We arrived at Yuma at eight the next morning and were told to take fifteen minutes to get a cup of coffee while the train took on water. We saw camps of Yuma Indians along the Colorado River, then passed by the mountain of white sands and a salt mine, too. We traveled all day, and finally the train pulled in to Los Angeles about half past four in the afternoon. An officer at the station asked whether we were the party going to General Miles's headquarters, and I said, "Yes, sir." He bade me and the others to fol-

Fort McDowell, northeast of modern-day metropolitan Phoenix, in 1921. Mike Burns was living here at the time, having reunited with members of his family.

low him, and soon we got into an ambulance. He asked me how long we had been on the road, and I said that it must have been four days since we left the San Carlos Agency. "So you must be the Apaches?" he asked. I said we were.

We got to headquarters, and we had a long talk with General Miles. He said that he would send us home in a few days, but that if we had a mind to we could go to the ocean or to Santa Monica. The ambulance took us to the beach, and we sat there at ebb tide and watched the people running around gathering seashells.

Two days later General Miles asked Captain Coffee what he wanted, and the chief replied that he wanted to get back to his home-land to farm the river bottom and raise crops to live on. General Miles asked him where he wanted to relocate, and Captain Coffee said that there were some families living just above the mouth of the Gila River on the Colorado River. He said that the Indians had been living there for a long time growing corn, wheat, barley, watermelons, pump-kins, and many other foods, and they got along with the white people around them just fine. He said that the Indians were free to do as they pleased, and some of the young ones even worked in the mines and got paid the same as any laborer. So he wanted the government to let him go back to that country.

General Miles told us that we could return to Fort Yuma the next day, and then go up to the Gila River to look the valley over and visit the people there to see if it would be all right. Then we were to go back to Willcox and Fort Grant, and thence to the San Carlos Agency.

We went on the eastbound train to Yuma, where some Mojaves met us and helped us get to the Yuma camp. We reached the home of the headman, where I received word that I had to go back to headquarters again to meet some Apache Mojaves. So I got on the train and went back to Los Angeles and waited nearly a week until Lieutenant Watson's party arrived. The lieutenant had made reports about the country and the land that he considered good for farming, and the number of families that might make their homes there.

General Miles asked which chiefs wanted to go there. Some of the chiefs had stayed behind at Fort Mohave, and Coquannathacka spoke up and said that for the A, C, D, and E bands he wanted the land near Camp Verde, up on Clear Creek and the headwaters of Beaver Creek, especially just below Montezuma Well, and also on Oak Creek and at Cottonwood. General Miles said that he would make a request recommending that the people be allowed to go to their original homes. He would have to send this to the president of the United States and the secretary of the interior for their consideration, and he could not say when he would get a reply, because everything had to go through the Indian Office.

No one should say anything unless he knows the facts. General Crook ought not to have made such promises unless he knew that he had the power to do as he wished. General Miles told the people he would do all in his power to have the government consent to send the Mojaves and Yumas to Fort McDowell and the Verde Valley, and General Miles said that he would also send a letter to the agent at San Carlos to let the people know when they would be moving to their former homes. General Miles told me to go home to San Carlos, and he told the rest of the Indians to do the same.

On the way to San Carlos, Lieutenant Watson asked whether anyone knew anything about the white man who had been killed on the San Pedro River. Chief José said no, that his men had been out there but were only looking for mescal to eat. Lieutenant Watson remained suspicious until a scout who had served with General Crook for twenty-five years told him that he had never known Chief José to tell a lie, and that he should not be blamed for what someone else had done.

Chief José said that he was not afraid to return to the San Carlos Agency. Everyone was eager to move back to their homelands, remembering that they had fought the enemies of the United States to win them back. But Captain Pierce said that he could not say just when they could move, because the papers had to go to the president to be signed into law. He said in time all Indians would have to look out for themselves, and do as they wanted without being told to do this and that, and live and progress among the white people, not on the reservation.

I was still doing duties as a scout and interpreter when a big council of the Mojaves and Yumas was called. A runner had come to the agency saying that a party of Indians had killed a white man on the San Carlos River across from an Indian camp. About fifteen scouts went out with Lieutenant Watson and a detachment of soldiers. We made camp at the headwaters of Deer Creek, below the Coal Field, and the next morning we came to the place where the man had been killed. The body of the dead man had been burned, and the place too, and we could get no trace or track of any kind, since all kinds of animals had been there since. Some white men showed us the place where the shooting had taken place. They said that a stranger had come to the settlement and got the Indians drunk, and then they went off and shot this man. Nearly all the Indians had left the place and gone back to San Carlos.

We scared around the country to find trails to follow, but to no avail. After about three days we followed the old wagon road back to the Gila River. There was another Indian camp at the mouth of Dripping Spring Wash. The lieutenant wanted to march on it, but before we reached the river an Indian woman told us that the camp had been vacated. Lieutenant Watson asked her if she had heard about the killing over on the San Pedro River, but she said that she knew nothing about such things. The lieutenant ordered us to continue on to the camp and keep an eye on her.

When we arrived at the camp we found corn drying on the roofs, and wheat and barley growing. Lieutenant Watson ordered us to search the houses to see whether we could find anything belonging to that white man. We ransacked every tepee, but we found nothing belonging to any white man. Still, it looked strange that the people had left so suddenly and left so many valuables behind; they might have done the murder, or they might know something about it that they didn't want to tell us.

The next morning we followed their trail, which led over the Mescal Mountains and crossed a rough canyon. After a few hours we saw smoke curling up on the mountainside and two Indians leading ponies down from the top of the mountain. They didn't see us. We waited until they went down to where the smoke was coming from, then went over and looked over the edge of a steep gulch. There were quite a number of tepees. We waited for soldiers to come, but Lieutenant Watson ordered us to move right into the camp. This must have been about 10:00 in the morning. We moved on, and we noticed that the Indians didn't seem to mind us coming near them. We had been expecting a fight. When we got to the camp, Lieutenant Watson ordered everyone out to be counted. The chief came out and made a great speech, saying that he had been permitted to stay outside the San Carlos and White Mountain Reservations. He had a paper to prove it, he said; they had never harmed anyone and were allowed to stay on their own land. This had been going on for ten years, thanks to an agreement that General Crook had made when he was stationed there.

When I got back to the San Carlos Agency I joined the Indian scouts again, with Chief José's Yuma band. Sam Kill was the only one who did not join the scouts. In a month and a half Lieutenant Watson returned, again talking of Fort McDowell and the Verde River bottomlands. Captain Pierce, however, told the Indians that they all had to go back to their farms and work on digging ditches and building dams to irrigate the fields. It would be a while before word would come about moving. As soon as the Chiricahuas were subdued and there were no more Indian wars, and as soon as all the Apaches settled down to farm and live at peace with everybody, then we could go home.

It took another ten years for this to happen. Some of the Mojaves went to Camp Verde in 1898, and others went to Fort McDowell in 1902.

I stayed with the company until my six months' service expired. That was on January 26, 1886. That was the last of my government service.

Epilogue

Mike Burns ended his military employment on January 26 or January 27, 1886, ending a complicated and troubling episode in his life, an Indian at work hunting down other Indians in the service of the white conquerors of Arizona. He immediately fell on hard times, like so many residents of the San Carlos Agency. In September of that year, he appealed to General Miles to be returned to service, writing:

> I was discharged on the 27th of January last after serving the United States (6) months as an Indian Scout. Since then, I have engaged in choping wood and staying with relatives I have found among the Mohaves. The Indian ration is not the thing to work. It lasts but two and three days out of seven. It goes very hard with me, General, for I am not used to it. I have been with the Army since I was a child, and now there is no work to do, and [I] asked Capt. Pierce, the acting Ind. Agent, to be reenlisted, but I was told that the numbers of scouts allowed here are filled. I thought that you have the power to allow one more. As you are the only Officer who knows me and do me a favor. I am the one who met you at Leavenworth, Kansas, and departed for New Mexico. Please recommend me for a position above private.

Whether General Miles responded we do not know, but Burns never returned to military service. Instead, he continued to do odd jobs at San Carlos, marrying in about 1888 a young woman named Chehata, or Hattie, whose father was a prominent Tolkepaya—Apache Yuma, Burns would have written—leader. Mike and Chehata had six children: Solomon, Carlos, Katie, Charlotte, Lula, and Josie. From the elders in his extended family, who would have taught the children

A letter from
Mike Burns to
Gen. Nelson
Miles asking
to be reinstated
to service as an
Indian scout.

such things, Burns learned about Yavapai customs, traditions, and history, an education he had missed in his own childhood.

When the Yavapai people were finally allowed to return to portions of their homeland at the end of the nineteenth century, the Burns family went with them, moving first to Camp Verde, then to a small ranch near the mining town of Mayer, not far from Prescott. In 1913 he made his final move, to the Fort McDowell Indian Reservation on the Verde River northeast of Phoenix, the home of only a few hundred Yavapais, recently ravaged by an outbreak of tuberculosis. He remained there for the rest of his life, returning to his boyhood home of Fort Whipple only in illness. It was there, on November 26, 1934, that he died.

Mike Burns had long been in correspondence with historian Sharlot Hall, among others whom he hoped to enlist in publishing his work, which he seems to have begun writing years before. He introduced himself to Hall in 1910, writing, "I am an Apache Indian of this Territory and received a little education at Carlisle Indian School of

[The same
letter, p. 2]

Penna. Will you give me the address of a man or a magazine to whom I can send letters about a little history of the Apaches? And including my own history." Hall encouraged Mike to tell his story, and he energetically worked on it for many years, writing to his distant cousin Wassaja, or Carlos Montezuma (see page 41), on January 7, 1913, "I am going to tell the White People that they have heard only one side of the stories about how bad the Apaches were to the whites. But the Apaches were forced to be so and they tried to protect themselves, their homes and their land. And who would not do the same thing?"

Burns's efforts eventually informed the histories of ethnologist E. W. Gifford and historian Thomas Edwin Farish, but he published only a few short articles under his own name. Part of the reason for his lack of success may have had to do with his idiosyncratic prose style, a representative sample of which is this:

> All then head men of the different band talked about what best
> to do and all decided to come within a weeks time. But in the

meantime some of their young men were out hunting deer and antelops happen to noticed great lines of horsemen at some distance and came to notify the rest. Most all the Indians broke camp and moved down towards the Verdi river: kindly some other directions from where the soldiers were heading. So these three new men returned to Camp Verdi to tell General Crook that in 4 or 5 days there will be a great number of Indians will come in. They assured them that when the camp Indians starts from their camp they will start up some smokes of fire and that the soldiers must meet them a few miles from the post.

More likely, however, Burns's ethnicity impeded his efforts to publish, for it would be decades before Native American voices entered the historical narrative of the Indian Wars, a narrative dominated by military officers and pulp writers. Burns discovered this in 1922, when

Mike Burns at about the age of seventy. This is the last known photograph of Burns.

he gave a copy of his manuscript to William H. Corbusier, the surgeon who had served at Camp Date Creek and who had long been a sympathetic student of Kwevkepaya lifeways. Corbusier carefully edited Burns's manuscript, although, as befit his time, he removed most of Burns's pointed charges against the Anglo invaders. Several publishers rejected the resulting book as being of no interest to general readers—and this at a time when western novels and histories were widely popular, so long as they were told from the victor's point of view.

Burns continued to send letters to Sharlot Hall, asking for her help in publishing his memoir. There are no copies of her replies in Burns's archives, but he was evidently encouraged, for in the spring of 1929 he delivered a draft of the book you are now reading. Hall seems to have edited a few of the pages, but, so far as we know, she made no real effort to move the manuscript toward publication. Instead, Burns's memoir sat in the archives of the Sharlot Hall Museum in Prescott, Arizona, for decades afterward, occasionally visited by scholars writing on Arizona history, occasionally incorporated here and there into children's books and magazine articles, its pages jumbled and misordered but otherwise unread.

Publication, then, has been a long time coming, and we must hope that the time is finally right for Mike Burns to find the many readers he deserves. His words speak to us across the generations from a document unlike any other in the history of the Southwest.

Notes

The map in this book was drawn by Gene Hall. All photographs are taken with permission from the archives of the Sharlot Hall Museum in Prescott, Arizona, with the exception of the photograph of Four Peaks on page 9 and of the Verde Valley on pages 20–21, which are by Gregory McNamee, and the photograph of Gen. George Crook on page 46, which is from the National Archives. Documents quoted in these notes that are without specific citations are also from the archives of the Sharlot Hall Museum and may be consulted there.

vi   "the most signal blow ever received by the Apaches in Arizona": Bourke, *Diaries*, 51.

ix   "the narrator was allowed": Opler, *Apache Odyssey*, 6.

ix   "Opler also observed": Opler, *Apache Odyssey*, 224.

ix   "So much has been written of the Indians": Farish, *History of Arizona*, 288.

1   "I belonged to an Apache Indian family": Throughout his autobiography, Burns refers to himself as an Apache, as the Yavapai people were collectively called during the nineteenth century. The misnomer was applied by Americans who had trouble distinguishing the Athapaskan-speaking Apaches from their mountain- and desert-dwelling neighbors to the west. The Yavapais, variously called "Apache-Mojaves," "Mojave Apaches," "Apache-Yumas," "Yuma Apaches," "Tonto Apaches," and so on, fell into four main groups: the Kwevkepayas, Mike Burns's people, who lived along the Verde River and whose territory extended southeast to the Pinal Mountains around Globe; the Tolkepayas, who lived in the plateau and desert country between the Bradshaw Mountains and the Colorado River; the Yavapes, who lived in the area around Prescott and the Hassayampa River drainage; and the Wipukepas, who lived north of the Verde River between the Mazatzal Mountains and the Mogollon Rim.

1   "cave on the north side of the Salt River": The place is called Skeleton Cave, so named for the material remnants of the fight that Burns describes. The Salt River lies about nine hundred feet below the cave, which is extremely difficult to reach. For this reason, the Kwevkepayas considered it a prime sanctuary.

1   "The place is on the north side": Mike Burns believed that he was born at
    Fish Creek, the place the Kwevkepayas called Gagattavalva, "Steep Pass."

1   "The Four Peaks were white with snow": The Four Peaks, at 7,657 feet in
    elevation, lie at the southern end of the Mazatzal Mountains near present-
    day Roosevelt Lake. They are important in the practical and sacred geog-
    raphies of several Native American groups in Arizona.

1   "I was taken to an officer": James Burns, born in Ireland, immigrated
    to the United States and soon thereafter, on July 28, 1858, enlisted as a
    private in the Fifth Cavalry. He served in the Civil War, after which he
    was promoted to lieutenant and then posted to Arizona.

2   "I can only guess that I was born in 1864": Some sources give 1862 as
    Mike Burns's birthday, which would have made him ten at the time.

2   "she was pulled out and shot many times": William Corbusier, an
    army doctor who edited a much-expurgated and never-published ver-
    sion of Burns's memoirs, protests, "Our troops never intentionally shot
    at women and children, but at long range could not always distinguish
    them from the men. They always sympathized with their captives and
    shared their rations with them. They would take the disabled ones and
    the small children who were unable to walk on their horses, just as Mike
    was taken by Captain Burns. Probably other Indians were in the bushes
    and Mike's mother was mistaken for a man." It is for the reader to judge
    which account is the more accurate.

2   "old Fort Grant on the San Pedro River": Originally established as Fort
    Arivaypa, Camp (then Fort) Grant was first located within Aravaipa Can-
    yon, then in 1872 relocated to the east of the canyon, away from the San
    Pedro River. The original post was the site of the Camp Grant Massacre
    of March 1871; see pages 143–144.

3   "General George Crook, who was commanding the Department of Ari-
    zona": George Crook (1829–90) is considered one of the fairest-minded
    of the senior military commanders in the Indian Wars. Most of his long
    service in the military was spent in the West; his training fighting in
    California served him well while fighting Confederate guerrillas in the
    Cumberland Mountains of Tennessee during the Civil War. His bravery
    and efficiency led to his promotion to general over several senior officers,
    which caused them no end of resentment and would trouble his later
    career. Writes biographer Dan Thrapp, Crook "was sincerely interested
    in the welfare of the Indians and in justice to red and white alike; he was
    intrepid, of generally noble sentiments and his influence is felt to the pres-
    ent day in Indian-white relations" (*Encyclopedia of Frontier Biography*, 350).
    Crook will figure prominently in Burns's memoir.

3   "Indian Territory": The Indian Territory comprised what is now Oklahoma.

3   "Captain Burns himself died": For details of Captain Burns's death, see
    page 81.

4   "the great chief Delshe": In much of the contemporary literature and

some later historical accounts, Delshe is identified as a Tonto Apache, but the Kwevkepayas considered him one of their own.

4 "so that the soldiers could not see them": Modern historians, using recently established forensic evidence, reckon the Yavapai dead at Skeleton Cave to number seventy-six. Writing to his cousin Carlos Montezuma in 1912, Burns recounts, "About that 'Salt River Cave Massacre' I could not truthfully say just exact number Indians were killed but I only got the number from the soldiers. Because I could not count anything at that time nor did I went to see to everyone was killed. That is, I think, unreasonable for anyone to state the exact numbers were seen dead in that cave. Good many were on top the others and were mashed so it could not tell whether a whole or pieces of human flesh. Because they were crushed by large rocks; from above the caves about five or six hundred feet high."

The belief that Delshe's band was "annihilated" there dates from military reports that used the word, apparently with reference to dead warriors alone; by that account, since all the men at the cave were reportedly killed, the Kwevkepaya band was indeed annihilated. Delshe himself, however, survived. Another Kwevkepaya leader, Nanni-Chaddi, did not, and Burns may be confusing the two.

4 "like he was dragging a log": Captain Burns, however, told Dr. Corbusier that Mike "fought, bit and scratched like a tiger" when he was captured.

4 "he died like a man": Burns's account agrees in many particulars with that of John Gregory Bourke in *On the Border with Crook* (187–201). Bourke, who was present at the fight, characterized it, however, as a two-sided affair. He adds that his men took positions above the cave and rolled boulders down onto it, crushing many of the Indians below, after which his troop advanced. "I hope that my readers will be satisfied with the meagrest description of the awful sight that met our eyes," Bourke writes. "There were men and women dead or writhing in the agonies of death, and with them several babies, killed by our glancing bullets, or by the storm of rocks and stones that had descended from above. While one portion of the command worked at extricating the bodies from beneath the pile of debris, another stood guard with cocked revolvers or carbines, ready to blow out the brains of the first wounded savage who might in his desperation attempt to kill one of our people. But this precaution was entirely useless. All idea of resistance had been completely knocked out of the heads of the survivors, of whom, to our astonishment, there were over thirty" (198).

6 "in the year 1872": The attack took place on December 27, five days after Burns's capture. On Christmas Day, Mike Burns, according to a diary entry by John Gregory Bourke, "gave an account . . . of three rancherias— one . . . in a cañon on Rio Salado, and 3rd on top of the four peaks." In a report dated December 30, 1872, Captain Bourke states that he "took the Tonto boy and had him tell Maj Brown's Apache soldiers where the

rancheria was and then Maj Brown & I concluded to combine both commands and go for the place" (Bourke, *Diaries*, 65). There had been earlier reports of a Yavapai settlement at a cave, but the fact that it was so quickly found suggests that Mike Burns did in fact reveal the location under duress.

Daklugie, a Mescalero Apache, recalled years afterward to the historian Eve Ball, "The victims of that massacre were not of my tribe, but they were Apaches [*sic*]. That was after Crook was brought back to the Southwest to exterminate the Apaches. I have been to that place while there were still bones of my brothers to be seen. There are some who think that one man lived to escape, but I do not know whether or not that is true. If so, that was still extermination of a band" (*Indeh*, 78).

7   "the only one of our three large families": See pages 1–2.

7   "tore down the wigwam": More likely a wickiup.

11   "the Superstition Mountains near the Gold Field": Goldfield was a mining town founded in about 1892 on the site of a gold claim. It lies at the base of the Superstition Mountains near the present city of Apache Junction.

11   "We found a mescal kiln": Mescal is an alcoholic beverage made by distilling agave in a kiln, similar to tequila and bacanora. The drink had uses in some ceremonial contexts and was an important trade good, but it was also the source of much trouble. The agave waste was also eaten.

12   "Silver King": Founded in 1877, Silver King is now a ghost town near Superior.

14   "Lieutenant Schuyler and Al Sieber were in charge": Albert Sieber was born in Germany on February 29, 1844. His family emigrated during the revolutionary unrest of 1848, settling first in Lancaster, Pennsylvania, and then in Minnesota. Sieber served in the First Minnesota Infantry during the Civil War and fought at Antietam, Fredericksburg, and Gettysburg. After the war he worked as a prospector and rancher in California and Arizona, then signed up with Gen. George Crook's command as a scout. In 1872 Crook named him chief of scouts, a position he held until 1887, when he was relieved following the Apache Kid incident (see pages 145–151). Sieber died while prospecting near Burns's birthplace on February 19, 1907, crushed by a falling boulder. Some scholars hold that the death was not accidental but that instead Apaches working on a road crew nearby exacted vengeance for crimes done to their people.

15   "Eskiminzin": The name of this Aravaipa Apache leader is usually rendered so. John P. Clum, a contemporary chronicler, spelled it "Es-kin-in-zin." In Apache it is Haski'banzin, meaning "Angry Men Stand in Line for Him" or "Anger Stands beside Him."

16   "Captain Pierce": F. E. Pierce was superintendent of the San Carlos Agency from 1885 to 1888.

20   "Coyote Hole": This will become a significant place in the geography of Burns's narrative. See pages 149–153.

25   "near the country around Gila Crossing": Gila Crossing, where the Salt and Gila Rivers join, was in Akimel O'odham (Pima) territory.

25   "near the Harquahala country": The Harquahala Mountains lie about a hundred miles to the west of Phoenix.

26   "near the confluence of Ash Creek": The confluence of Ash Creek and the Agua Fria River is near present-day Cordes Junction, on Interstate 17 north of the Black Canyon.

26   "His name was Townsend": John Benjamin Townsend (1835–73) was proud to be described as an "Indian killer," even though, as Burns notes here, he was half Cherokee. Born in Tennessee and a Confederate veteran of the Civil War, he moved to Texas, where Comanches killed several members of his family. This appears to have engendered a thirst for revenge extended to all Indians, and when Townsend settled in Arizona in 1863 he delighted in killing any Indian he encountered. The citizens of Prescott awarded him a Henry rifle with a silver plate on it engraved with the words "Honor to the Brave." Townsend served as a scout under Gen. George Crook until he reportedly scalped fifteen Indian prisoners after a fight at Squaw (now Piestewa) Peak, near Phoenix. Crook dismissed him. His death at Dripping Springs, which Burns describes, was marked by a funeral in Prescott that hundreds attended.

30   "Echawamahu": See pages 148–152.

34   "Townsend was in the gang": See pages 26–29.

36   "A party of white men": This reference may be to the Walker Expedition of 1863, led by Joseph Reddeford Walker (1789–1876), though Burns's details are sketchy. Bawoleuna may be a mangling of Paulino or Pauline, the first name of the Weaver whom Burns will soon mention, though Burns seems to consider them separate people.

38   "This massacre took place": Will Barnes, in *Arizona Place Names*, puts the naming of Skull Valley at 1864, writing, "There was a fight here . . . between a bunch of soldiers under Lieut. Monteith and some Mohave and Tonto Apaches. They left without burying the dead Indians. Later on Major Willis sent a scouting party out which found and buried the dead whose bones and skulls were lying round everywhere. Major Willis then named it Skull Valley" (410). Other sources put the fight in 1866.

38   "a white man named Lehi": Burns's reference is to Indian affairs superintendent C. W. Leihy, who was killed by renegades on November 10, 1866, near Kirkland Junction.

39   "The Oatman family": Royce Oatman and his wife and children were traveling alone along the Gila River near present-day Painted Rocks State Park in February 1851 when they were attacked by Indians, variously identified as Apache Yumas or Tonto Apaches. The adults and a baby were killed, while fourteen-year-old Lorenzo was badly hurt and left for dead.

The two girls, Olive and Mary Ann, were taken captive. Olive, the tattooed girl whom Burns refers to, was ransomed two years later, while Mary Ann died in captivity. The story was a cause célèbre in its day. For more, see Mifflin, *The Blue Tattoo*.

39   "he was General Howard": Oliver Otis Howard (1830–1909) was the chief commissioner of the Freedman's Bureau, under the auspices of which he founded Howard University in Washington, D.C., in 1867. Soon afterward he was posted to lead the campaign against Cochise's band in Arizona. He made a treaty with Cochise that was quickly broken on his reassignment to Oregon and Idaho, where he oversaw the relocation of the Nez Perce under Chief Joseph to a reservation.

41   "he is now a doctor in Chicago": Carlos Montezuma, a Tolkepaya, was born near Four Peaks in the Superstition Mountains in about 1866, only a few years after Mike Burns's birth. He was captured by Pimas and sold to a trader named Carlos Gentile, who gave him his name. Gentile later settled with Montezuma in Chicago, and Montezuma earned a medical degree at Northwestern University. He became a prominent activist for Native American rights though the journal he founded, *Wassaja*. He died at the Fort McDowell Indian Reservation in 1923.

45   "The other four": Burns's math is off, and one chief seems to have disappeared from the count.

47   "Hualapai chief Surauma": Sherum or Surrum, a Hualapai warrior, fought against federal troops during the Hualapai War, which began in 1865 over a treaty dispute. An outbreak of disease decimated the Hualapais, who surrendered in 1868.

47   "the first camp they reached was Walapai Charlie's": Walapai Charlie was a tribal leader who lived near Kingman. He refused to participate in the Ghost Dance movement, which Burns will later describe (see pages 148–152), and for this he lost some influence among his people.

53   "the headwaters of Oak Creek": The headwaters of Oak Creek lie on the Mogollon Rim below Flagstaff, at the head of Oak Creek Canyon. The stream flows past Sedona, the red rock country Burns alludes to.

55   "Supai country": That is, the present-day Havasupai Indian Reservation in the western part of the Grand Canyon.

56   "toward the Mogaume Mountains": Presumably, Burns means the Mogollon highlands and the Gila River.

61   "the place where so many Indians were killed": That is, Skull Valley. See pages 37–38.

61   "Lieutenant Charles King": Charles King (1844–1933) left school at sixteen to enlist in the Union army. President Abraham Lincoln awarded him a cadetship at West Point, and he graduated with honors near the end of the Civil War. As a first lieutenant he was transferred to the Fifth Cavalry on December 31, 1870, and assigned to Fort Verde, Arizona. He was seriously wounded in the fight described here, which took place on

November 1, 1874, at Sunset Pass in Coconino County. Burns's account, however, is considerably different from that of King, who dismissed the scouts as "Apache-Yumas whom I did not know at all and whom [my second lieutenant] could not especially recommend." See Cozzens, *Eyewitnesses*, 2:172.

King retired on medical disability but returned to service during the Spanish-American War, serving in the Philippines and attaining the rank of major general. He retired, finally, in 1931 after seventy years of military service. Along the way he wrote more than sixty books, including *Campaigning with Crook* (1890).

65   "chief named Charlie Chapan": Charlie Chapan was also called Charlie Pan.

66   "was sent to Florida with them": Apache prisoners of war, notably the followers of Geronimo, were sent to Fort Marion and other posts in Florida and Alabama to thwart efforts by their fellow Apaches to liberate them.

67   "the man who had freed the Negro people after having a war between the South and the Northern people": Burns is confusing Ulysses S. Grant with Abraham Lincoln, but in an interesting way.

67   "the third was Motha, Fog": Burns also calls Motha "Cloud."

70   "when they learned of his death": General Crook died in Chicago on March 21, 1890, at the age of sixty.

74   "they found some of their men wounded, as well as two white men": Corbusier reports: "A Special Commissioner, T. L. Dudley, from Washington was taking these Indians (1400) to San Carlos and Lieut. George O. Eaton, Fifth Cavalry, with fifteen enlisted men was along as a guard for the Agency people, who were camped between the unfriendly tribes when on March 8, 1875, the Apache Yumas and Apache Mojaves charged through our camp up on to a low mesa, dropped on their knees and fired a volley at the Tontos. Lieut. Easton charged up the mesa and stopped the fight. No white men and no women or children were wounded. I saw only four dead ones and dressed the wounds of ten Indians. There may have been a few others."

77   "Dr. Washington Matthews": Like James Burns, Washington Matthews (1843–1905) was born in Ireland. Raised in Iowa, he became a medical doctor and joined the army in the closing years of the Civil War. He remained in the army as a surgeon and was posted to several western camps and forts. He was an amateur botanist and ethnologist as well, and his writings on the Hidatsa and Navajo peoples are still studied today, especially his book *The Night Chant: A Navaho Ceremony*, which appeared in 1902.

80   "in the mountains behind Squaw Peak": Squaw Peak, near Phoenix, is now called Piestewa Peak, named for a young Hopi woman killed in the Iraq War in 2003.

81   "He died after crossing the Little Colorado River": Dr. Corbusier writes,

"Captain Burns died just after we had made camp on the afternoon of August 15, 1874, about seventy-five miles west of Fort Wingate."

81   "Captain John G. Bourke": John Gregory Bourke (1846–96) ran away from home at the age of sixteen to enlist in the Fifteenth Pennsylvania Cavalry. As a private he received the Medal of Honor for his gallantry in action at Stone River, Tennessee. In 1865 he received an appointment to the United States Military Academy and became an officer on graduation. He joined the Third US Cavalry and served for many years as aide-de-camp to Brig. Gen. George Crook. Fluent in Greek, Latin, Irish, and Spanish, Bourke learned several Apache dialects and wrote extensively about Native American culture. His books *An Apache Campaign* (1886) and *On the Border with Crook* (1891) are important accounts of military life on the western frontier. Brilliant though he was, Bourke was repeatedly passed over for promotion. Just two weeks before his fiftieth birthday, on June 8, 1896, Bourke died of a ruptured aneurysm.

84   "Lieutenant Charles King": On Charles King, see pages 61–64.

85   "Sergeant Logan had saved his life": Burns appears to have confused the name, for it was Sgt. Bernard Taylor who was awarded the Medal of Honor for rescuing Lieutenant King.

87   "the journey to Pueblo, New Mexico": The geography suggests that Burns means Isleta Pueblo, about thirteen miles south of Albuquerque.

87   "Colonel Wesley Merritt": Wesley Merritt (1834–1910) served as a general in the US Army during the Civil War and Spanish-American War. During the Indian Wars, with the lesser rank of colonel, he distinguished himself as the commander at the Battle of Slim Buttes (see pages 101–105).

89   "a man named Frank Grouard": The story of François Grouard (1850–1905) is one of the more curious in western frontier history, as this report from a Honolulu newspaper, the *Kuakoa*, of September 30, 1876, relates:

> A Hawaiian by name of Frank Grouard is living as a scout in the American Army under General [George] Crook, fighting Sioux Indians. Let us read his touching story and consider the way he has overcome the misfortune that befell him.
>
> Frank Grouard is a native of Honolulu, the principal city of the Hawaiian Archipelago, who as a youth worked as a sailor aboard ship in the Pacific. In 1865 he was living in San Francisco working as a mail guard between California and Montana.
>
> During one of his trips on a lonely trail he was captured by Crow Indians and taken prisoner. The Crows took him many miles from the road, and in a lonely forest, stripped off his clothes and possessions, then released him to wander alone.
>
> He wandered, cold and hungry, a piece of fur for clothing, eating grasshoppers and other bugs for food. When he had given up hope of

surviving, he was discovered by a group of Sioux Indians. Because of his expressions of aloha, they took a liking to him.

The Sioux took him into a heavily forested area where he was cared for. Chief Sitting Bull adopted him to be his own child of his own blood but with a different language. He grew in stature to be greatly admired by the Indians for his skill and wit. It was as if he had truly become one of them.

In a very short time, he became one of the best riders of wild Indian horses and he became one of the best shots. He went on raids against Indian enemies. For nine years he lived with the Indians, his manner becoming much like them.

Then he escaped and met with the haoles [whites]. From that time he became a chief scout for the government for the pay of $10 per day. He is 24 [*sic*] years old and is the most trusted scout of General Crook.

91   "the first time I ever rode on a railroad train": On pages 41–44 Burns relates that he took a train journey east in 1870, so there is some confusion in his writing here that this was his first train trip.

92   "Our scouts were Frank Grouard and Bill Cody": William F. "Buffalo Bill" Cody was born in LeClaire, Iowa, in 1846. After leaving home at the age of eleven, he herded cattle, worked as a driver on a wagon train, and engaged in fur trapping and gold mining. He was briefly employed as a military scout, in which capacity he appears here. Soon afterward he founded the Wild West Show, a staple of popular entertainment in the 1870s, and became an advocate of Indian rights. He died near Denver in 1917.

96   "until the Indians went away": Note that Burns's math in this description only adds up to six.

99   "crossed over into the British Possession": The British Possession is Canada, which was ruled by Great Britain until devolution and independence took place during the late nineteenth and early twentieth centuries.

103   "Yellow Hand": Burns writes "Yellow Ham." This account of Yellow Hand's death varies wildly from other contemporary records.

107   "Belle Fourche River": Burns calls the Belle Fourche River "Bill Fuse Creek."

110   "ordered to Fort Brown": Fort Brown was renamed in 1878 to honor Chief Washakie, who negotiated the treaty establishing the Wind River Reservation. It was a center for the African American cavalry units called the Buffalo Soldiers in the late 1800s. Burns spells Washakie's name Waskakai.

110   "they were worth $4.75": In a separate document Burns puts the value of the gold at $7.64.

115   "where the Utes had killed Agent Meeker": The Meeker Massacre oc-

curred on September 29, 1879, near present-day Meeker, Colorado. Agent Nathan C. Meeker had been trying to convert the Utes from hunters to farmers, and he plowed up a racetrack in order to prove his power. The owner of the racetrack and Meeker scuffled, and Meeker sent to the army for help. Maj. T. T. Thornburgh brought a detachment of two hundred soldiers to the Ute Agency. At Milk Creek, Utes ambushed the column, and Thornburgh and all his officers above the rank of captain were cut down. The Utes then returned to the agency and killed Meeker and seven other whites. Chief Ouray (see the following note) apparently ordered the Utes to stop fighting as soon as news reached him of these events, but a great outcry among white settlers soon forced the removal of the Utes to a new reservation in Utah.

115   "where Chief Ouray gave himself up": Chief Ouray (1833–80) was the leader of the Uncompahgre band of the Utes. In 1868 he signed a treaty with President Grant giving the San Luis Valley of Colorado to his people. The treaty was broken when a gold rush was touched off in the nearby San Juan Mountains. The Meeker Massacre, in Rio Blanco County, was one consequence. After negotiations for a new reservation, President Rutherford B. Hayes called Ouray "the most intelligent man I've ever conversed with." See Elias, *Colorado*, 39.

118   "The owner was a man named Mr. Valentine": Lawson Valentine, among other things, was an important patron of his partner's brother, the painter Winslow Homer.

122   "the great Brooklyn Bridge": The Brooklyn Bridge was completed in 1883.

124   "stop fighting and become good people": It is not clear whether Burns is being ironic in his talk in this paragraph of good Christians, but the suggestion is that he is.

125   "Rulo, Nebraska": For Rulo, Burns writes "Lulo City."

126   "Professor McCarty": Hugh De France McCarty (1822–99) was a school superintendent, teacher, and early educational leader in Doniphan County, Kansas. Born in Pennsylvania, he moved to Leavenworth, Kansas, in 1857, served as a Union officer in the Civil War, and then became a professor of chemistry and president of Highland University.

129   "he can beat old Carver": Carver was evidently the company marksman.

142   "Captain Snook, who was the first sergeant": Snook, a Tolkepaya, was actually a corporal. He was well known for his enmity toward Tonto Apaches.

144   "to make a treaty": Burns's account of the incident that history knows as the Camp Grant Massacre, which took place on April 30, 1871, is substantially correct. Eight men and more than a hundred women and children, most of them Aravaipa Apaches, were slaughtered by a combined force of Mexican and Tohono O'odham fighters organized by Tucson civic leaders William Oury and Jesús María Elías, who blamed all depredations in southern Arizona on Eskiminzin's band.

150   "at Cassadore's camp": Cassadore was a leader of the San Carlos Apache band and an ally of Geronimo. His name is a familiar one at San Carlos today, and his descendants are numerous.

151   "drunk on tizwin with whiskey mixed in": Victor Randall, a Mescalero Apache, once remarked to historian Eve Ball, "A *tiswin* drunk? It wasn't *tiswin* that usually caused the trouble. We didn't have enough corn to make *tiswin*. It is not distilled; it's just fermented and about as strong as beer. It takes a lot of drinking to get drunk on *tiswin*. When you read about these *tiswin* drunks, just remember that they were mostly whiskey or tequila drunks" (*Indeh*, 296).

153   "Charlie Pan was the head chief": Whites pronounced the name of Es-chetlepan, a Tonto leader, as "Chalipun" or "Charlie Pan."

153   "did not care to have them back in that part of the country": In 1887 a delegation of Yavapai County farmers, ranchers, and officials wrote to President Grover Cleveland, "We deem it a great wrong and injustice to have [Yavapais and Tontos] located among us as . . . we cannot live here with any safety for we know from their previous actions, they cannot be contented for only a short time no matter where they are. Their only ambition is to murder, steal, and plunder. Now if they are to move here there is only one thing left for us to do, that is to sacrifice what we have."

155   "some families living just above the mouth of the Gila River": These families living along the Gila River were the Castle Dome Tolkepayas, who lived in the Castle Dome Mountains not far from the confluence of the Gila and the Colorado, near present-day Yuma. They grew summer crops on the bottomlands but understandably preferred to live in the mountains for protection.

References

Ball, Eve. *Indeh: An Apache Odyssey.* Provo, Utah: Brigham Young University Press, 1980.

———. *In the Days of Victorio: Recollections of a Warm Springs Apache.* Tucson: University of Arizona Press, 1972.

Barnes, Will. *Arizona Place Names.* Tucson: University of Arizona Press, 1989.

Barrett, S. M. *Geronimo: His Own Story.* 1906. New York: Meridian, 1996.

Bourke, John Gregory. *The Diaries of John Gregory Bourke,* vol. 1. Edited by Charles M. Robinson III. Denton: University of North Texas Press, 2003.

———. *On the Border with Crook.* 1891. Lincoln: University of Nebraska Press, 1971.

Braatz, Timothy. *Surviving Conquest: A History of the Yavapai Peoples.* Lincoln: University of Nebraska Press, 2003.

Corbusier, William Henry. *Soldier, Surgeon, Scholar: The Memoirs of William Henry Corbusier.* Edited by Robert Wooster. Norman: University of Oklahoma Press, 2003.

Cozzens, Peter. *Eyewitnesses to the Indian Wars, 1865–1890,* 2 vols. Mechanicsburg, Pa.: Stackpole Books, 2001.

Elias, Megan. *Colorado: The Centennial State.* Milwaukee: World Almanac, 2002.

Farish, Thomas Edwin. *History of Arizona,* vol. 3. San Francisco: Filmer Brothers, 1916.

Goodwin, Grenville. *Western Apache Raiding and Warfare.* Edited by Keith H. Basso. Tucson: University of Arizona Press, 1971.

Heitman, Francis B. *Historical Register and Dictionary of the U.S. Army, 1789–1903.* Urbana: University of Illinois Press, 1965.

Hinton, Leanne, and Lucille Watahomigie, eds. *Spirit Mountain: An Anthology of Yuman Story and Song.* Tucson: University of Arizona Press, 1984.

Jacoby, Karl. *Shadows at Dawn: A Borderlands Massacre and the Violence of History.* New York: Penguin Press, 2008.

King, Charles. *Campaigning with Crook.* 1890. Norman: University of Oklahoma Press, 1964.

Mattina, Anthony. *The Golden Woman: The Colville Narrative of Peter J. Seymour.* Tucson: University of Arizona Press, 1985.

Mifflin, Margot. *The Blue Tattoo: The Life of Olive Oatman.* Lincoln: University of Nebraska Press, 2009.

Opler, Morris. *Apache Odyssey*. New York: Holt, Rinehart and Winston, 1969.

Shepherd, Jeffrey P. *We Are an Indian Nation: A History of the Hualapai People*. Tucson: University of Arizona Press, 2010.

Tate, Michael L. *The Frontier Army in the Settlement of the West*. Norman: University of Oklahoma Press, 1999.

Thrapp, Dan. *Encyclopedia of Frontier Biography*, vol. 1. Lincoln: University of Nebraska Press, 1991.

About the Editor

Gregory McNamee is the author of more than thirty books, including *Gila: The Life and Death of an American River* and *Otero Mesa: Preserving America's Wildest Grassland.* The son of a career military officer, he has written extensively about historical subjects for many publications, among them *Native Peoples* and the *Washington Post.* He is a contributing editor and consultant in world geography to the *Encyclopaedia Britannica,* a contributing editor to *Kirkus Reviews,* and a contributing editor to the *Bloomsbury Review.* McNamee is a research associate at the University of Arizona Southwest Center and serves on the adjunct faculty of the Department of Economics at the University's Eller College of Management.